The Great Music Trivia Quiz Book

The Great Music Trivia Quiz Book

Rachel Federman

HarperCollins*Publishers*

HarperCollins*Publishers*
77-85 Fulham Palace Road,
Hammersmith, London W6 8JB

www.harpercollins.co.uk

First published by HarperCollins*Publishers* 2009

10 9 8 7 6 5 4 3 2 1

© Rachel Federman 2009

Rachel Federman asserts the moral right to
be identified as the author of this work

A catalogue record of this book is
available from the British Library

ISBN 978-0-00-732468-2

Printed and bound in China
by Leo Paper Products

▶ Acknowledgements

To Jeannine, for all she contributed to this book and for returning from London.

Thanks to: Kristine and the Laddomadas, Matt "Decca Records was huge" Santarpia, Baby Ray, Baby Angie, Erica "Burning Down the House" Heisman, Casey Hallas, Plaza Toros, the Billy Riordan Band, Poppy and his saxophone, Guitar Joe for loving music so much he could not live without it and Bayonne Joe for once having been that way, Dara and the girls for keeping Moon Rocks alive, and my parents for raising us in a house full of music with speakers bigger than our living room.

▶ Contents

▶ Introduction

They believed in magic. They could see for miles.
They had many rivers to cross. And so, as soon as
the musical trailblazers of the past sixty years
were old enough to leave wherever it was they
didn't want to be anymore, they followed the
siren call of melody and rhythm that told them to
walk on the wild side. Whether you listened to the
phonograph, the radio, the hi-fi, the stereo, a
walkman, or an iPod—or watched their concerts
live—then you heard that same call. As popular
music gave a voice to each generation's need to
break away from the past, chart-topping hits,

experimental basement tapes, dance-floor favorites, and arena-shaking rock shows turned everyday moments into epic scenes of hope and love, loss and wonder.

Most of all our favorite musicians gave us a place to put feelings so urgent and all consuming that they couldn't merely be spoken aloud, trapped on paper, or hung in a museum. They could only be airborne, traveling the way they had for thousands of years, on waves of sound, across our yards and gardens like a cup with a string to our best friend's house, then further, across miles, oceans, and the ages. For many, great songs have been a life force, the most direct and universally understood answer to the question "How do you feel?" A reason (we just asked for one) to keep dreaming on.

In the trivia questions that follow, ranging from the years of bebop and swing before rock 'n' roll, up through the decades of doo-wop, protest songs, punk and indie rock, metal, hip hop, Britpop, and rap all the way to the present, you'll find the stories behind the bands, the real people behind the magazine covers, the breakthrough hits, the secret muses, the one-hit wonders, the bizarre cover versions, the record-breakers, the weirdest misheard lyrics, before-they-were-famous factoids, B-side esoterica, and major turning points in this ethereal world of operatic splendor, seedy tabloid fodder, and everything in between. There's even a section for true music geeks (the ones who can, for example, read actual music). Multiple-choice and true-or-false questions, fill-in-the-blanks and matching games will help you prove just how much of an expert you are on everything—from Chuck Berry's signature walk to U2's original name to the song Beyoncé performed at the 2009 Presidential Inaugural Ball.

At the end, check your answers against the back of the book, tally up your points, and, if you believe in the gospel of music, you'll find out just how good a shot at redemption you have. Maybe you'll end up mystified and struggling for answers. If so, you're in the right place too. Music has always lured us out of our comfort zones and traditions with the promise of adventure and escape, if only we're willing to let that screen door slam. We may not know where we'll wake up the next morning, but we hope it will be to the sound of music with someone named Mary hovering over us, speaking words of wisdom. But if the words don't come, don't worry. You don't really need them. As long as you listen to the music, you'll get what you need.

The Quizzes

Ready?
Go!

▶ Pre-rock 'n' roll

(15 questions)

Was there life before rock 'n' roll? In some form, yes, just like there was life before the Neolithic Revolution, 10,000 years ago, that allowed humans to settle down in one place. What did people listen to and was it any good? Well, like the eternal debate over whether R.E.M.'s *Green* album represented the beginning or the end of their brilliant contribution to alternative music, it depends on whom you ask. There are those who believe humans have never come close to the achievements of the eighteenth century in music and those who can't fathom needing more than three chords and the truth. In the twentieth century alone, however, jazz, swing, big band, gospel, blues, folk, country, and bluegrass all did more than merely entertain. They brought people together, told stories, broke boundaries, and paved the way for a musical revolution.

1. Which orchestral piece, composed by Sir Edward Elgar, is played at almost every graduation in the United States?

_____

Points: 1

2. Long before heavy metal, industrial or goth, which movement from New Orleans (which gave rise to such greats as Duke Ellington and Louis Armstrong) was initially marginalized as "the Devil's music"?

_____

Points: 1

3. Match the artist with the genre:

Swing	Bessie Smith
Baroque	Joan Baez
Bebop	Johann Sebastian Bach
Classical	Charlie Parker
Folk	Glenn Miller
Blues	Joseph Haydn

Points: ½ point for each correct match

4. Chuck Berry, considered by many to be the father of rock 'n' roll, was famous for walking while playing guitar in a way that resembled which animal?

_____

Points: 1

5. Which type of record has the longest playing time?

a) **LP (Long Play)**
b) **EP (Extended Play)**
c) **single**

Points: 1

6. George Gershwin is famous for his Rhapsody in what color?

a) **Ruby**
b) **Indigo**
c) **Blue**
d) **Yellow**
e) **Marigold**

Points: 1

7. The first Gold Record award was given in 1942 to which artist to celebrate over one million sales of "Chattanooga Choo Choo"?

Points: 2

8. Which U.S. city was given the first commercial FM license in the country in 1941?

a) Nashville
b) Chicago
c) New York
d) San Francisco
e) St. Louis

Points: 2

9. Frustration with Irving Berlin's "God Bless America" inspired Woody Guthrie to write the lyrics to this famous protest song in 1944. (Hint: Picture the Redwood Forest.)

Points: 1

10. "White Christmas" (which songwriter Irving Berlin is known to have modestly called "the best song that anybody's ever written") was a hit single for Bing Crosby and is naturally associated with the 1954 movie of the same name. But the song that became the world's greatest-selling single came onto the scene quietly in a 1942 film, also starring Bing Crosby. What was it called?

a) *Country Girl*
b) *Blue Skies*
c) *Going My Way*
d) *Holiday Inn*
e) *High Time*

Points: 2

11. Thomas Edison's phonograph, the first machine capable of storing sound, used a cylinder wrapped in what common household material?

a) wax
b) paper towel
c) tin foil
d) plastic wrap
e) linoleum

Points: 1

12. The first collaboration between Rodgers and Hammerstein resulted in this 1943 musical named after a state "where the wind comes sweepin' down the plain." Which one is it?

_____

Points: 1

13. What was the longest-running musical on Broadway in New York City?

_____

Points: 3

14. What was the longest-running musical in London's West End?

_____

Points: 3

15. Who did Frances Ethel Gumm play in *The Wizard of Oz* (1939)?

_____

Points: 2

Pre-rock 'n' roll score ___/25

▶ 1950s

(10 questions)

The babies were booming, the singers were crooning, the suburbs were expanding, and— in the beginning at least—parents knew where their children were: up in their bedrooms listening to Doris Day. James Dean was a rebel without a cause, Marlon Brando was the wild one, and Frank Sinatra, pied piper for the lonely-hearted, starred in *From Here to Eternity*. Sure there were distant fears of alien invasion and nuclear war, but things were falling apart in other places, as

Chinua Achebe's exposé of Nigeria poetically showed.

When Elvis broke onto the scene with his scandalous hip shakes and jailhouse rock, the establishment didn't know what had hit it. Kids idolized convicted felons and social outsiders like Chuck Berry and Jerry Lee Lewis. Wherever it was Sam Cooke wanted to be sent, parents didn't want to know. Still, three years later, when the times really were a-changin', those same parents would give their eye teeth to know all they had to worry about was a teenager in love exhausted from one-too-many-nights spent rocking around the clock.

1. The Weavers made it a number one hit in 1950, but Huddie "Lead Belly" Ledbetter recorded the original version of this haunting lullaby of sorts nearly two decades earlier. What was it called?

"_____, Irene"

Points: 2

2. This 1956 release from 20th Century Fox about two brothers during the American Civil War was Elvis Presley's first foray into cinema. The film's original title—*The Reno Brothers*—was changed to the title of the first single when the advance music sales went through the roof. What is the name of the movie (and the single)?

a) *Viva Las Vegas*
b) *Blue Suede Shoes*
c) *Are You Lonesome Tonight?*
d) *Love Me Tender*
e) *Return to Sender*

Points: 2

3. The day in February 1959 when Ritchie Valens, the Big Bopper, and Buddy Holly died in a plane crash was dubbed "The Day the _____ _____" by Don McLean in his eight-and-a-half minute 1971 hit "American Pie." (The radio single was cut in half.)

_____

Points: 1

4. Name the movie from which the following quote comes and the character who said it.

After a high-energy performance of "Johnny B. Goode" at a mid-1950s high school dance:

"I guess you guys aren't ready for that yet. But your kids are gonna love it."

Movie: _____

Character: _____

Points: 1 for each correct answer

5. The capital of the Caribbean island of Jamaica was the inspiration for which successful pop/folk trio, who hit it big with their versions of "Where Have All the Flowers Gone?" and "Tom Dooley"?

Points: 2

6. Johnny Cash's song "Five Feet High and Rising" refers to what memory from his childhood?

a) working in the family cotton fields
b) the Arkansas floods
c) the lifelong dreams Johnny had of witnessing his older brother Jack (killed in a horrific mill accident) ascend to heaven
d) neighborhood bonfires
e) growing up with the Christian faith

Points: 2

7. At a mid-50s performance at the Apollo Theater in New York's Harlem, the sensationalist performer of "I Put A Spell on You" fame was supposed to spring out of a coffin but got locked inside. Who was he?

Points: 3

8. True or false?
Elvis had a fraternal twin brother who died before birth.

Points: 2

9. The inspiration for the name of the 1980s New Wave group The Pretenders came from the song "The Great Pretender" by which soulful R&B group that hit it big in the 1950s?

a) **The Four Aces**
b) **The Playmates**
c) **The Chantels**
d) **The Platters**
e) **The Teen Queens**

Points: 2

10. Country cross-over star Patsy Cline wasn't crazy about this song when it was presented to her, but her 1957 version soared up the pop charts, keeping people up late into the night to listen.

a) **"Walkin' After Midnight"**
b) **"In the Midnight Hour"**
c) **"Round Midnight"**
d) **"Lady Midnight"**
e) **"Midnight Confession"**

Points: 2

1950s score   */20*

▶ 1960s

(41 questions)

Charles Dickens' best of times and worst of times described late eighteenth-century Paris and London, but it could easily apply to the 1960s, a decade which promised so much (literally, the moon) but exacted an enormous toll at the same time as it delivered on those promises. The American President, John F. Kennedy, was shot in Dallas before he finished his first term. There was a giant leap for mankind, but the hope that springs eternal was dampened by the threat of a silent spring. Still, Martin Luther King had a dream and millions believed in it.

There were battle calls and sit-ins, marches, and rallying protest songs. There were mini skirts and screaming fans for the lads from Liverpool who started out wanting to hold your hand and ended up in times of trouble. Some teenagers kept right on twisting again like they had the summer before, asking Buttercup to build them up, others were lighting someone's fire, telling people to get off of their cloud, or hoping the world would give peace a chance.

By the end of the decade, the war in the Pacific had expanded, The Beatles had broken up, Dylan had gone electric, then country, and JFK, MLK, and RFK were all long gone. Two years later, Hendrix, Janis, and Morrison would be as well. Maybe you really needed more than love. Once the purple haze had cleared, those who'd been so eager to leave their comfortable homes and gather 'round some great unknown and powerful force, were probably more than willing to admit that the waters around them had grown.

1. It's a restaurant on East 52nd street in Manhattan, a concerto by Antonio Vivaldi, and a group from the 1960s who scored big with hits like "Big Girls Don't Cry" and "Stay." What is it?

a) **The Four Seasons**
b) **The Ace of Cups**
c) **Cupid's Inspiration**
d) **The Balloon Farm**
e) **Bull & the Matadors**

Points: 1

2. What does "TCB" stand for in Aretha Franklin's 1967 hit "Respect" (written and originally sung by Otis Redding)?

_____

Points: 2

3. Diana Ross has two stars on the Hollywood Walk of Fame. One is for her solo work and the other is for her participation in which Motown act that began as a sister group to The Primes?

a) **The Temptations**
b) **The Marvelettes**

c) **Gladys Knight & the Pips**
d) **Dreamgirls**
e) **The Supremes**

Points: 1

4. Roy Orbison's 1964 chart-topper about a pretty woman reached a new generation through the 1990 feature film blockbuster. It's often left off, but the song's title actually has a third word in it. What is it?

_____

Points: 1

5. How many years passed between the release of Jimi Hendrix's first album "Are You Experienced" (1967) and his death in Notting Hill, London?

a) 1
b) 3
c) 5
d) 9
e) 15

Points: 2

6. Which band was not part of the original "British Invasion" (1964 to 1966)?

a) **The Animals**
b) **The Rolling Stones**
c) **Freddie and the Dreamers**
d) **The Cure**
e) **The Kinks**

Points: 1

7. Davy Jones from Manchester, England is best-known for his role in one of the world's first "boy bands" (also a TV show from 1966-8). What were they called?

Points: 1

8. Country music star Dolly Parton first performed at the Grand Ole Opry at the age of:

a) **9**
b) **13**
c) **18**
d) **21**
e) **25**

Points: 1

9. To which band does the following August 1964 quote in the *Daily Mirror* refer?

"These performers are a menace to law and order, and as a result of their formula of laryngitis, cranial fur and sex the police are diverted ... to quell the mob violence they generate."

a) **The Beatles**
b) **The Rolling Stones**
c) **The Doors**
d) **Cream**
e) **The Dave Clark Five**

Points: 2

10. What record company did Dick Rowe, "the man who turned down The Beatles," work for when he auditioned the group from Liverpool on New Year's Day in 1962?

a) **Warner Brothers**
b) **Decca Records**
c) **Epic Records**
d) **Roulette Records**
e) **Imperial Records**

Points: 2

11. "Soul Brother Number One," "The King of Funk," and "The Godfather of Soul" all refer to which legendary twentieth-century entertainer?

a) **Stevie Wonder**
b) **James Brown**
c) **Ray Charles**
d) **Marvin Gaye**
e) **Howard Tate**

Points: 1

12. Romantic Poet William Blake's line "If the doors of perception were cleansed everything would appear as it is, infinite" inspired the name of which boundary-breaking trio from Los Angeles whose albums include *Strange Days*, *Waiting for the Sun*, and *Morrison Hotel*?

_____

Bonus: The bluesy-psychedelic rockers mentioned above played *without* this rock 'n' roll staple in their live shows. What was it?

a) guitar

b) drums

c) bass

d) keyboards

e) organ

Points: 1 + Bonus: 1

13. In the U.K., which album from 1967 is the all-time best-selling record? (This will be no surprise to those who enjoyed the show.)

_____

Points: 1

14. Three days before he died, Otis Redding recorded this song, which he co-wrote and originally called "The Dock of the Bay." What was it ultimately called?

_____

Points: 1

15. Which 1960s duo originally called themselves Tom and Jerry (no relation to their actual names)?

_____

Points: 2

16. Who is the only rock star to win an honorary Pulitzer Prize for a "profound impact on popular music and American culture, marked by lyrical compositions of extraordinary poetic power."

a) John Lennon
b) Paul Simon
c) Bob Dylan
d) Pete Seeger
e) Leonard Cohen

Points: 2

17. Which member of The Beatles is barefoot on the cover of *Abbey Road*?

_____

Points: 1

18. How old was the oldest Beatle when Paul McCartney announced he had left the band in April 1970?

a) **38**
b) **35**
c) **31**
d) **29**
e) **25**

Points: 1

19. Which band established itself as the entertainment during "Acid Test" parties in 1960s San Francisco?

a) **Big Brother & The Holding Company**
b) **Moby Grape**
c) **Jefferson Airplane**
d) **The Great Society**
e) **The Grateful Dead**

Points: 2

20. True or false?

a) For a short time The Rolling Stones called themselves "The Rollin' Stones"

_____

b) Ed Sullivan demanded that the Stones change their lyrics to "Let's spend some time together" as opposed to spending the night together

_____

c) The Rolling Stones got their name from the Bob Dylan song

_____

d) The Stones' first single was "I Can't Get No Satisfaction"

Points: 1 point for each correct answer

21. Only one of this groundbreaking performer's songs ever made it to the charts. Who is he?

a) Jimi Hendrix
b) Bob Dylan
c) Eric Clapton
d) Marvin Gaye
e) Otis Redding

Points: 2

22. The cover version of which of these songs was released in advance of Bob Dylan's original version?

a) "All Along the Watchtower" (Jimi Hendrix)
b) Just Like Tom Thumb's Blues (Nina Simone)
c) "I Threw It All Away" (Yo La Tengo)
d) "Just Like a Woman" (Richie Havens)
e) "Tambourine Man" (The Byrds)

Points: 2

23. In the mid-1960s, Jimmy Page was given the chance to replace Eric Clapton in an English blues-rock band. He declined at that time, but later joined the outfit; what was it?

a) **Cream**
b) **The Yardbirds**
c) **The Who**
d) **The Animals**
e) **Fabulous Thunderbirds**

Points: 2

24. Who were the first act to perform on the other side of the iron curtain? (Maybe it's because they were able to live up to their name.)

a) The Beatles
b) Rush
c) The Bee Gees
d) Blood, Sweat & Tears
e) The Monkees

Points: 1

25. How much would a three-day pass for the 1969 Woodstock Festival have set you back? (Hint: The minimum wage in the U.S. was $1/hour.)

a) **Nothing**
b) **$5**
b) **$18**
c) **$43**
d) **$98**

Points: 2

26. Smokey Robinson chose the names Tamla and Berry for his kids as a tribute to Berry Gordy, the founder of Detroit's Tamla Records, which in 1960 changed its name to the one we use today. What is it?

Points: 2

27. Where is Jim Morrison buried?

a) **Miami, Florida**
b) **London, England**
c) **Los Angeles, California**
d) **Paris, France**
e) **New Haven, Connecticut**

Points: 2

28. A broken ankle and a back injury forced Jimi Hendrix to leave …

a) **Little Richard's tour**
b) **a position in Joey Dee and the Starlighters**
c) **the Army Airborne**
d) **a job selling tickets to a local circus act**
e) **a horseriding championship**

Points: 2

29. Ike and Tina made it famous, but which rock band led by John Fogerty wrote "Proud Mary" and included it on their 1969 album *Bayou Country*?

Points: 1

30. The Scottish singer-songwriter Donovan of "Season of the Witch" fame has a limp as a result of which disease? (He was infected after a childhood vaccination.)

a) measles
b) tuberculosis
c) polio

e) cholera

Points: 2

31. In Wilson Pickett's "In the Midnight Hour"
there's an instrumental after the second
verse. Which instrument is featured in the
solo?

a) guitar
b) piano
c) drums
d) horn
e) organ

Points: 3

32. Which word comes right before the guitar solo in Janis Joplin's "Piece of My Heart"?

a) good
b) baby
c) tough
d) it
e) indeed

Points: 3

33. Which song from Simon and Garfunkel's 1968 *Bookends* did both Yes and David Bowie cover? (Hint: If you're lost, ask Kathy.)

a) "America"
b) "Old Friends"
c) "Mrs. Robinson"
d) "A Hazy Shade of Winter"
e) "Save the Life of My Child"

Points: 1

34. Which notorious "Helter Skelter" criminal lived with the Beach Boys' Dennis Wilson in 1968?

Points: 2

35. In the dance-floor favorite "Oh, What a Night" (The Four Seasons), which month and year was that infamous night? (Hint: It's also an alternate name for the song.)

Points: 1

36. At what enormous summer of love event in upstate New York did Neil Young first play with Crosby, Stills, Nash & Young?

Points: 1

37. Although it's hard to imagine "Knockin' on Heaven's Door" without Axl Rose wailing out "doh-wa-woor" the song was originally played acoustically and written for the 1973 Western *Pat Garrett & Billy the Kid* by which artist?

a) Bryan Ferry
b) Bob Marley
c) Muddy Waters
d) Bob Dylan
e) Paul Simon

Points: 2

38. Where did The Beatles first set foot on U.S. soil (in February of 1967)?

_____

Points: 2

39. In "British Invasion" band The Kinks' song "Rosie, Won't You Please Come Home" who is Rosie?

a) **Ray's girlfriend**
b) **Dave's ex-girlfriend**
c) **Rose Kennedy**
d) **Ray and Dave's sister**
e) **the "Woman with a Rose" in a print by Zoltan Glass**

Points: 2

40. Guitar Al Kooper from Blood, Sweat & Tears jumped in on an impromptu organ performance for the 1965 recording of which Bob Dylan song (the first song on *Highway 61 Revisited*)? (Hint: His inexperience on the instrument led to an ⅛-note delay on each chord, a quirky addition with which Dylan famously fell in love.)

Points: 2

41. At a party thrown after Janis Joplin's fatal heroin overdose in 1970 and according to instructions in her will, the invitations read "Drinks are on _____," her nickname and the name of her posthumous and best-selling album.

_____

Points: 2

Score ___/69
Bonus ___/1
1960s Total ___/70

 1970s

(44 questions)

The 1970s are best known for coming after the 60s and before the 80s. As far as music goes, no unifying theme persists. From the smiley faces and lava lamps, bellbottoms and hot pants, you'd think everyone was still feeling groovy. Maybe it was because Watergate, a recession, the oil embargo, and the arms race gave young people plenty of reason to want to get down tonight, especially Saturday night, escaping into the disco fever that took over dance floors across a nation bent on stayin' alive. Space exploration kept on truckin', bringing back pieces from the dark side of the moon, as did advances in Women's Rights and the environmental movement. Millions hoped for a peaceful easy feeling so they could stand up and say, "I'm okay, you're okay."

Musically, there was a lot happening in the 70s. While the Boss went around preaching the gospel of rock and roll, the Steve Miller Band played their music in the sun, and Neil Young searched for a heart of gold. Angry kids cranked up the distortion and screamed their disdain for the establishment. Their 60s counterparts had strummed acoustic guitars and hoped for freedom, but these punk rockers wanted anarchy, in the U.K. and everywhere else. At the same time, heavy metal was coming into its own, taking head-banging angry teens in through the out door down a highway to hell. Was it too much, too little, too late? There was more than a feeling, but maybe not more than enough to override the excessive glare from the disco balls and sequined crop-tops in a decade whose identity crisis is best summed up by ghetto fabulous white boys saying "I dig," wearing leisure suits, and otherwise keepin' it real.

67

1. Where is The Stone Pony, the music club that opened in 1974 where Bruce Springsteen launched his Born in the USA Tour? (Hint: The name of the city appears in one of his album titles.)

Points: 1

2. When Duane Allman of The Allman Brothers Band and Bonnie Raitt used glass medicine bottles while playing guitar, what effect were they going for?

a) bending
b) hammer on
c) sweep picking
d) slide guitar
e) crashing

Points: 1

3. What night in September did Earth, Wind & Fire ask if we remembered in their 1978 "ba de ya" hit?

a) 1st
b) 8th
c) 15th
d) 21st
c) last day

Points: 1

4. This award-winning singer-songwriter was famous for "Leaving on a Jet Plane" and in October of 1997, off the coast of

California, that is in fact, how he left. Who was he?

a) **Steve Gaines**
b) **Stevie Ray Vaughn**
c) **Jim Croce**
d) **John Denver**
e) **Randy Rhoads**

Points: 1

5. Both Jefferson Airplane and Queen have a song titled "Somebody to Love." Which group uses multiple tracks of the vocals to create a gospel choir sound?

Points: 1

6. Before he sold the world in 1970, this glam rocker from Brixton, London sometimes went by the stage name Davie Jones or Davy Jones, but should not be confused with the vocalist from Manchester's "Daydream Believers" (a.k.a. The Monkees). Who is he?

Points: 1

7. John Travolta performs this dance in *Saturday Night Fever*; the album by the same name was a hit record in 1975 by Van McCoy and the South City Symphony. What is it?

Points: 2

8. Which song and album won Grammys for Best Pop Song, Record of the Year, and Song of the Year in 1970? (Hint: It will ease your mind.)

Points: 1

9. Why was Billy Joel unable to graduate from high school?

a) He was offered a deal with Columbia Records
b) He was drafted
c) He joined the Echoes
d) He overslept and missed an exam
e) He got into a dispute with his music teacher

Points: 1

10. Which artist has the greatest number of R&B/hip hop hits? (Hint: She has also won 15 Grammys, the highest number ever awarded to a female performer.)

_____

Points: 1

11. Which album by The Who features Big Ben on the front cover (on the U.S. release only)?

_____

Points: 2

12. Which English punk rock musician was arrested for killing his girlfriend Nancy Spungen in New York's Chelsea Hotel and died less than half a year later, at age 21?

a) **Johnny Rotten**
b) **Mick Jones**
c) **Barrie Masters**
d) **Sid Vicious**
e) **John O'Neill**

Bonus: What was the number of the room at the Chelsea Hotel in which Nancy Spungen was killed?

Points: 1 + Bonus: 1

13. Fill in the song titles from these 70s hits.

a) Walk on the _____ Side (Lou Reed)
b) I Can _____ Clearly Now (Johnny Nash)
c) _____ Softly with His Song (Roberta Flack)
d) The Way We _____ (Barbra Streisand)
e) _____ Mr. Postman (The Carpenters)

Points: 1 for each correct answer

14. What is the name of a synthesizer worn around the neck, as popularized by Ohio's electronic outfit, Devo?

Points: 1

15. Which two Queen albums (1975 and 1976) share their names with Marx Brothers movies?

_____   _____

Points: 1 for each correct answer

16. One of four co-writers of Starship's 1985 hit "We Built This City" is the English singer/songwriter best-known for his decades-long creative partnership with Elton John. Who is he?

_____

Points: 1

17. What 1973 show marked the end of The Everly Brothers' harmonious relationship?

_____

Points: 2

18. The songs by this Belfast musician are among the most popular choices for movie soundtracks and were included in *Proof of Life*, *Born on the Fourth of July*, *An Officer and a Gentleman*, *Sleeping with the Enemy*, *The Outsiders*, and *Wonder Boys* along with many others. Who is he? (Hint: His fans know him as "_____ (his first name) the Man.")

_____

Points: 1

19. What was the ratio of men to women in the New York Dolls?

Points: 1

20. For Alice Cooper's original 1972 release of *School's Out* the vinyl record came wrapped in:

a) women's underwear
b) a kerchief
c) a football jersey
d) swimming trunks
e) a skull cap

Points: 1

21. At a 1988 tribute show for Nelson Mandela's 70th birthday which guitar legend joined Dire Straits for an eleven-minute version of their 1978 hit "Sultans of Swing"?

a) Jimmy Page
b) Johnny Marr
c) Eric Clapton
d) Slash
e) Neal Schon

Points: 1

22. Which now-closed New York music club did The Ramones partly own?

a) **CBGBs**
b) **Coney Island High**
c) **The Cooler**
d) **Meow Mix**
e) **Rocket to Russia**

Points: 1

23. This "rock poetess" was photographed by Robert Mapplethorpe, made "Because the Night" (co-written with Bruce Springsteen) famous, and collaborated with R.E.M. on "E-Bow the Letter" in the mid-1990s. Who is she?

a) **Stevie Nicks**
b) **Joni Mitchell**
c) **Carole King**
d) **Patti Smith**
e) **Carly Simon**

Points: 1

24. Derek and the Dominos' blues-rock classic "Layla" (1970) was written for Pattie Boyd who later became Eric Clapton's wife. To whom was she married at the time the hit was written?

a) **George Harrison**
b) **Mick Jagger**
c) **Jeff Beck**
d) **Tom Petty**
e) **Robbie Robertson**

Bonus: When writing "Layla," Eric Clapton was inspired by a book by the Persian poet, Nizami. What was the book's title?

Points: 1 + Bonus: 1

25. During the opening track to this landmark concept album you can hear the sound of a helicopter, a creepy laugh and a roadie muttering that he's been "mad" for a very long time. What is the name of the album?

a) *Pronounced Leh'-nerd Skin-'nerd* (Lynyrd Skynyrd)
b) *Led Zeppelin III* (Led Zeppelin)
c) *Rumours* (Fleetwood Mac)
d) *Machine Head* (Deep Purple)
e) *The Dark Side of the Moon* (Pink Floyd)

Points: 1

26. The distinctly funky sound on "Superstition," a hit single from Stevie "Boy" Wonder's (he was 22 when this record was released) *Talking Book* was achieved with what kind of keyboard made by Hohner?

a) **electric piano**
b) **clavinet**
c) **mellotron**
d) **pipe organ**
e) **analog synthesizer**

Points: 1

27. Who were the king and the queen of the prom in Billy Joel's "Scenes from an Italian Restaurant" (1977)?

Points: 1

28. These three brothers born on the Isle of Man won the Grammy for Album of the Year for their "Saturday Night Fever" soundtrack. What was the name of their pop-rock outfit which lasted forty-five years (until one brother died in 2003)?

Points: 1

29. In ELO's 1976 "Do Ya" what traditional song does the crowd sing in the moonlight?

a) "America, the Beautiful"
b) "Oh Shenandoah"
c) "Auld Lang Syne"
d) "Amazing Grace"
e) "Danny Boy"

Points: 2

30. True or false?
Two people served jail time for stocking Sex Pistols "Never Mind the Bollocks ... Here's the Sex Pistols" in their stores.

Points: 1

31. Although epic live versions of the song are known to go on endlessly, how long was the original track of Lynyrd Skynyrd's 1974 hit "Free Bird"?

a) **5:03**
b) **9:06**
c) **12:17**
d) **23:51**

Points: 1

32. Although it's also the name of a Swedish canned fish company, the name of this hugely popular band hailing from Sweden is actually an acronym of the first names of the four band members. Gimme, gimme, gimme the name of the band. (Hint: The name is the same if you read it backward or forward.)

_____

Bonus: Name the four band members.

_____   _____

_____   _____

Points: 1 + Bonus: ½ for each correct answer

33. When this legendary band reconvened in 1988 for the Atlantic Records 40th Anniversary, Jason Bonham, the son of the former (deceased) drummer, filled his dad's spot. What does the second word of the band's name mean?

a) **moving air**
b) **rocks**
c) **day of rest**
d) **airship**
e) **red**

Points: 1

34. The 1978 film *The Last Waltz*, documenting the goodbye concert of The Band at San Francisco's Winterland Ballroom, was directed by which director/artiste whose oeuvre of music-driven films includes *Mean Streets*, *New York, New York* and *No Direction Home: Bob Dylan*?

a) **Francis Ford Coppola**
b) **Woody Allen**
c) **Martin Scorcese**
d) **Oliver Stone**
e) **Spike Lee**

Points: 1

35. The Counting Crows brought the song about parking lots taking over paradise to generation-X-ers, but more than two decades earlier Joni Mitchell had written and released "Big Yellow Taxi" on her 1970 album *Ladies of the Canyon*. A visit to which U.S. state inspired the song?

a) **California**
b) **Hawaii**
c) **Maine**
d) **Arizona**
e) **Utah**

Points: 1

36. Which of the following names did Bruce Springsteen *not* consider when deciding what to call the era-defining album that became known as *Born to Run*?

a) *War and Roses*
b) *The Hungry and the Hunted*
c) *American Summer*
d) *Sometimes at Night*
e) *Hiding on the Backstreets*

Points: 3

37. True or false?

Pink Floyd's "Shine On You Crazy Diamond" from *Wish You Were Here* (1975) was written for Jim Morrison, lead singer of The Doors, who had died of an overdose four years earlier.

Points: 1

38. Fleetwood Mac is perhaps as famous for its changing lineup and rotating romances as for its music. Who is the only original member of the band still a part of the group?

a) **Stevie Nicks**
b) **Lindsey Buckingham**
c) **Mick Fleetwood**
d) **John McVie**
e) **Peter Green**

Points: 1

39. Which world-famous painter and filmmaker managed The Velvet Underground for a time and designed the yellow banana cover art for their first album (before running out the clock on his fifteen minutes of fame)?

a) **Edward Hopper**
b) **Roy Lichtenstein**
c) **George Segal**
d) **Andy Warhol**
e) **Lou Reed**

Points: 1

40. The same word is missing from the song titles of the 70s hits below. What is it?

"_____ Love" (Van Morrison)

"_____ On You" (Heart)

"_____ Train" (Ozzy Osbourne)

"_____ Little Thing Called Love" (Queen)

Points: 1

41. Some people attribute the first stage-dive to Peter Gabriel, but other sources credit the often-topless "Godfather of Punk" whose stage antics while part of The Stooges gained him notoriety even before he was officially a "Real Wild Child." Who is he?

a) Iggy Pop
b) Jim Morrison
c) Angus Young
d) Johnny Rotten
e) Lou Reed

Points: 1

42. In English, the title to Santana's electric 1971 hit remake of this song by Tito Puente means "What's up?".
What is it called?

_____

Points: 1

43. In what key is Led Zeppelin's classic and long-time high school dance-finale *Stairway to Heaven* written?

Bonus: At what point in the 8-minute ditty do the drums come in?

a) **At the start**
b) **About halfway through**
c) **There are no drums in the original recording**

Points: 1 + Bonus: 1

44. In the Bob Marley & The Wailers' breakthrough hit "No Woman, No Cry," do the song's title and refrain mean that

a) **you won't be upset if you don't have a woman (a similar if inverse conceit to B.I.G.'s "Mo Money Mo Problems" two decades later)**

or is he

b) **telling a woman not to cry?**

Points: 1

Score ___/55
Bonus ___/5
1970s Total ___/60

▶ 1980s

(49 questions)

After the sex, drugs, rock 'n' roll, and rallying calls of the previous eras, the 1980s saw the pendulum swing the other way. Forget gathering around a common cause—unless it was to start a not-so-quiet-riot. Girls wanted to have fun and boys fought for their right to party. Phil Collins made it big against all odds, The Police asked us not to stand so close, and Modern English wanted to stop the world and melt with you. We never stopped to think that the world itself might be melting, and that we might be the ones responsible.

In the 80s everyone was special (so special), and no one ever was to blame. Ronald Reagan felt he hadn't made enough bombs in Hollywood and stockpiled weapons for a real-life Star Wars. But the threat of nuclear annihilation didn't dampen spirits as much as one might have imagined. It may have been the end of the world as we knew it, but we all felt fine.

If we could have seen over the giant hair and shoulder pads, it would have been obvious that

104

Pac-man was no different from a big city banker; you won by gobbling up everything in your path. Salaries and housing values shot up way past where they belonged. We were pumping up the volume, looking forward to a thriller night, Wanging Chung—whatever the hell that meant, it didn't matter. Grown-up 1970s child wonder Michael Jackson said he was bad, but nobody believed him for at least another decade. So what if MTV killed the radio stars? It was a time when *The Golden Girls* and Cabbage Patch Kids reigned. By the end of the decade, we were free falling, about to be set loose into the world where the future was so bright that we had to wear shades.

105

1. What early 1980s album is the best-selling record of all time? (Hint: Eddie Van Halen played lead guitar on the third single released from this record.)

Points: 1

2. Joan Jett made "I Love Rock 'n' Roll" a hit in 1981, but it was written and originally released in the mid-1970s by Alan Merrill and Jake Hooker of what London-based pop outfit?

a) **Fleetwood Mac**
b) **The Village People**

c) Parliament
d) The Moody Blues
e) The Arrows

Points: 1

3. Which of the following musicians or groups are *not* from New Jersey?

a) Jon Bon Jovi
b) Bryan Adams
c) Kool and the Gang
d) Naughty by Nature
e) Whitney Houston

Points: 1

4. The first version of the *Purple Rain* screenplay was titled:

a) *I Only Want to See You*
b) *When Doves Cry*
c) *Dreams*
d) *Graffiti Bridge*
d) *Part Time Lover*

Points: 1

5. A ritual melody in the church, this is also the name of the first song on The Cure's 1989 album *Disintegration*.

a) "Disintegration"
b) "Pictures of You"
c) "Plainsong"
d) "Lullaby"
e) "Fascination Street"

Points: 1

6. You can find "(I've Had) The Time of My Life," "Love is Strange," "Hungry Eyes," and "She's Like the Wind" on the soundtrack to which 1987 film about a romance in the Catskills?

a) *Dirty Dancing*
b) *When Harry Met Sally*
c) *Youngblood*
d) *The Breakfast Club*
e) *Moonstruck*

Points: 1

7. Name the original songs on which the following "Weird Al" Yankovic takeoffs are based.

a) **"Another One Rides the Bus"**

_____

b) **"I Love Rocky Road"**

_____

c) **"I Think I'm a Clone Now"**

_____

d) **"Fat"**

_____

e) **"Like a Surgeon"**

_____

Points: 1 for each correct answer

8. In 1986, Chris de Burgh was mesmerized by a lady in red, but what color is associated with the heartbreaker in this Psychedelic Furs' 1981 song which lent its name to a John Hughes film starring Molly Ringwald?

a) turquoise
b) purple
c) yellow
d) pink
e) blue

Points: 1

9. In the Culture Club's 1983 hit "Karma Chameleon," loving would be easy if this capricious person's colors were like those in the singer's dreams. What three colors did Boy George dream about?

_____   _____   _____

Points: 1 for each correct color

10. In "La Isla Bonita," what island did Madonna dream of "last night"?

a) **St. John**
b) **Puerto Rico**
c) **Maui**
d) **San Pedro**
e) **Corsica**

Points: 1

11. Born Georgios Kyriacos Panayiotou, this pop singer from London sang "Careless Whisper" and "Wake Me Up Before You Go-Go" as part of the duo Wham before launching out on his own. What name does he go by?

_____

Points: 1

12. When did compact discs first hit the market?

a) **1980**
b) **1982**
c) **1983**
d) **1987**
e) **1989**

Points: 1

13. In 1982, Princess Diana named this quintessential 80s group (part of the second wave of the British Invasion) her favorite band. Many agreed that the five members were fabulous. Who were they?

a) **Duran Duran**
b) **Tears for Fears**
c) **Culture Club**
d) **Depeche Mode**
e) **Bananarama**

Points: 1

14. The last song on Toto's 1982 Grammy-winning *Toto IV* was almost cut from the album, but it reached number one in the charts, the band's only song to ever do so. Which is it?

a) "We Made It"
b) "Make Believe"
c) "Africa"
d) "2 Hearts"
e) "Straight for the Heart"

Points: 1

15. Blondie made "The Tide is High" famous in 1980, but it was written years earlier by a Jamaican DJ. The cover version preserves the ska/reggae beat which puts the accent where in the title? (Pick all that apply.)

a) **1st word**
b) **2nd word**
c) **3rd word**
d) **4th word**

Points: 1

16. Many fans insist that "echo" in Echo & the Bunnymen referred to this piece of equipment, used to accompany the band before Pete de Freitas joined Liverpool's sugar-lipped New Wave rockers. What was it?

Points: 1

17. For Morrissey of The Smiths, every day is like what day of the week?

a) **Saturday**
b) **Sunday**
c) **Monday**
d) **Tuesday**
e) **Friday**

Points: 1

18. After he saw their funk metal band perform at CBGBs in New York, Mick Jagger helped which African-American foursome get a deal with Epic Records?

a) **Living Colour**
b) **Faith No More**
c) **Jane's Addiction**
d) **Wu-Tang Clan**
e) **Arrested Development**

Points: 1

19. Their 1981 debut album was called *Too Fast for Love*, but their drummer proved he wasn't too fast for the camera when fourteen years later his videotaped honeymoon exploits with Pamela Anderson reached more far-away places than the band members' tattoos. What is the name of the band and the drummer?

Band: _____

Drummer: _____

Points: 1 for each correct answer

20. Where did the name "Black Sabbath" come from?

a) the last day of creation according to the Old Testament
b) lyrics from the opening song on Slayer's *Show No Mercy* album
c) the midnight meeting of witches in *Macbeth*
d) a dream Ozzy Osbourne had while under the influence of hallucinogens
e) the Italian horror film *I Tre Volti Della Paura*

Points: 2

21. Who was Janet Jackson's reported first crush? (Hint: She might have dreamed she'd run into him at the Copa, Copacabana.)

a) **Lionel Richie**
b) **Neil Diamond**
c) **Bing Crosby**
d) **Barry Manilow**
e) **Dean Martin**

Points: 1

22. This megastar played Aunty Entity in the 1985 film *Mad Max Beyond Thunderdome,* which featured her hit song "We Don't Need Another Hero." Who is she?

Points: 1

23. What body part did Sting break when he and Stewart Copeland fought on a 1983 tour of the U.S.?

a) ankle
b) jawbone
c) wrist
d) ribs
e) nose

Points: 1

24. What do these acronym bands' names stand for?

a) R.E.M.

_____

b) ELO

_____

c) OMD

_____

d) UB40

_____

Points: 1 for each correct answer

25. When writing this song for the 1983 album *Can't Slow Down*, Lionel Richie contacted the United Nations in hopes of finding an African sentiment that would work in the breakdown, but he ended up making something up instead. The final lyrics, however, did include a word each in Swahili (*Karamu*), Caribbean (*Liming*) and Spanish (*Fiesta*). What is the name of the song?

Points: 1

26. Which star from the long-running TV sitcom *Friends* was pulled on stage to dance in Bruce Springsteen's 1984 "Dancing in the Dark" video?

a) Jennifer Aniston
b) Matthew Perry
c) Matt LeBlanc
d) Courtney Cox
e) Lisa Kudrow

Points: 1

27. The Pet Shop Boys made it a hit, but "Always On My Mind" had been recorded by which musicians below, before the British electronica duo got their hands on it? (Pick all that apply.)

a) **Elvis Presley**
b) **Willie Nelson**
c) **Otis Redding**
d) **Bob Dylan**
e) **David Hasselhoff**

Points: 2

28. Rank the following Madonna records in order of worldwide sales, best to worst.

1984 Like a Virgin
1986 True Blue
1989 Like a Prayer
1992 Erotica
1998 Ray of Light

Bonus: All of Madonna's albums reached the top 5 in the U.K. charts except one. Which?

Points: 3 + Bonus: 1

29. This drummer for British hard rockers Def Leppard lost his left arm in a car accident at 21, but he rigged up a drum set where he played the snare with a foot pedal and continued playing. Who is he?

a) **Mitch Mitchell**
b) **Tommy Aldridge**
c) **Max Weinberg**
d) **Tommy Lee**
e) **Rick Allen**

Points: 1

30. When Simon Le Bon is straddling the line, in discord and rhyme, he is hungry like what animal?

a) hippo
b) horse
c) dog
d) wolf
e) shark

Bonus: Where was the video shot for the 1982 Duran Duran song referenced in the last question?

a) **Rio de Janeiro**
b) **Sri Lanka**
c) **London**
d) **the Amazon rainforest**
e) **Costa Rica**

Points: 1 + Bonus: 1

31. Which iconic radio personality from Michigan signs off after his countdowns: "Keep your feet on the ground and keep reaching for the stars"?

Points: 1

32. Which of the following females did *not* play bass in their respective bands?

a) Tina Weymouth (Talking Heads)
b) Kim Gordan (Sonic Youth)
c) Kelley Deal (The Breeders)
d) Maya Ford (The Donnas)
e) D'arcy (Smashing Pumpkins)

Points: 2

33. On U2's 1987 album (named after a national park in California), what is the title of the first song?

a) "I Still Haven't Found What I'm Looking For"
b) "Where the Streets Have No Name"
c) "One"
d) "One Tree Hill"
e) "In God's Country"

Points: 1

34. What percentage of MTV videos depict either drinking or smoking tobacco?

a) **One-quarter**
b) **One-fifth**
c) **One-tenth**
d) **One-half**
e) **Three-quarters**

Points: 1

35. This eclectic British singer accused the writers of the film *Napoleon Dynamite* of stealing the name from him, since it was a pseudonym he used on his 1986 album *Blood and Chocolate*. He was born Declan Patrick MacManus but what does he usually call himself?

_____

Points: 1

36. The father of world-renowned drummer Stewart Copeland (best-known for his work with The Police) was in real law enforcement. What agency did he work for?

a) **the FBI**
b) **Her Majesty's Prison Service**
c) **the Coast Guard Police**
d) **the CIA**
e) **the Federal Bureau of Narcotics**

Points: 1

37. After winning a Grammy for Best New Artist in 1985 and becoming the first artist in history to have five top-10 singles from a debut album, this singer/songwriter really proved that Queens girls can handle anything … including wrestler "Captain" Lou Albano who played her angry father in this classic video. Name the artist and the video.

Artist: _____

Video: _____

Points: 1 for each correct answer

38. Which Debbie Gibson single spent the most time at the top of the charts?

a) **"Lost In Your Eyes"**
b) **"Foolish Beat"**
c) **"Electric Youth"**
d) **"Only In My Dreams"**
e) **"Say Goodbye"**

Points: 1

39. When the background vocals kick in on the 13th line of Air Supply's "Making Love Out of Nothing At All", what does the singer know is "fading?"

_____

Bonus: In the video for this dramatic 1983 hit, where is the couple headed?

a) home
b) a romantic restaurant
c) a high school football field
d) the airport
e) Paris

Absurd-over-the-top-you'd-have-to-be-crazy-to-know-this bonus: What is the speed limit on the sign that the car passes after the woman makes a U-turn?

Points: 1 + Bonus: 1 + Over-the-top-bonus: 4

40. What year did MTV first air music videos?

a) **1975**
b) **1979**
c) **1981**
d) **1985**
e) **1987**

Bonus: Name the month and day the first videos aired.

_____

Points: 1 + Bonus: 1

41. Which video did *not* air on MTV's inaugural day?

a) "Cruel to Be Kind" by Nick Lowe
b) "Iron Maiden" by Iron Maiden
c) "Brass in Pocket" by The Pretenders
d) "Take on Me" by a-ha
e) "Bring It All Home" by Gerry Rafferty

Points: 1

42. Don Henley ended the innocence for one 16-year-old when he invited her to his hotel room in 1980. He wrote about his disgust at the press for exposing his private life in this 1982 hit from *I Can't Stand Still*. What was the name of the song?

Points: 1

43. What does "LL Cool J" stand for?

_____

Bonus: What is the name of the album where LL Cool J appears on the cover as a boxer?

_____

Points: 1 + Bonus: 1

44. CBS records—home at various points in their careers to megastars such as Bruce Springsteen, Bob Dylan, Barbra Streisand, and Michael Jackson—was sold to what Japanese company in 1988?

a) Kyosho

b) Sony

c) Makita

d) Nissan

e) Tokyo Broadcasting System

Points: 1

45. The name of Australian heavy metal band AC/DC's 8th album, released in 1981, is a reference to the Latin greeting Roman gladiators would make to the emperor before a fight: *Ave Caesar, morituri te salutant.* What is the name of the album?

Points: 1

46. The 2.5-acre Central Park memorial for John Lennon—not far from The Dakota apartment building where he lived and was killed—is named for a 1967 Beatles' song, initially written for *Sgt. Pepper's Lonely Hearts Club Band* but released as a single instead (opposite "Penny Lane" on a double-A-sided 45). What is it called?

Points: 1

47. How many counts of four are there in Quiet Riot's 1983 version of "Cum On Feel the Noize" before the vocals start?

a) **0, vocals start right in**
b) 1
c) 2
d) 8
e) 12

Bonus: Oasis also covered this song as a B-side for their fourth single from (*What's the Story) Morning Glory?* What was the name of that single?

Points: 1 + Bonus: 1

48. Which of the following is *not* true of Bon Jovi's 1986 single "Livin' on a Prayer" from *Slippery When Wet*?

a) It features a key change
b) Jon Bon Jovi had to be convinced to include it on the album
c) Richie Sambora used a talk box effect
d) It was used as a promotional song in the 2004 Democratic presidential campaign
e) The video was the only one from *Slippery When Wet* shot entirely in color

Points: 1

49. Whitney Houston's anthemic "One Moment in Time" was written for what 1988 summer event held in Seoul, South Korea?

_____

Points: 1

Score ___/65
Bonus ___/10
1980s Total ___/75

▶ 1990s

(39 questions)

°

After the massive housing sprawl, endless greed, and increasingly superficial iconography of the glitz and glamour decade, the 90s were ushered in with a sweeping and collective "Now what?" The Red Hot Chili Peppers had a suggestion for what to do with all the excess—give it away. Poison hoped for something to believe in, but what? The Shiny Happy People? (Not.) The fire that we didn't start? Another day in chick flick paradise?

Early on in the decade, punk rock and heavy metal music were converging. Finally, Generation X-ers had found their answer to the nihilism and apathy left in the wake of the "me" decade. The disaffected hero at its center, Kurt Cobain, came from a little town called Aberdeen, wore black eyeliner, smashed his Fender Jaguars, and dated the lead singer of L.A.'s Hole. The music world was in a daze; they thought they'd found God.

As for the rest of the decade, Mariah Carey had a vision of love, Will Smith got jiggy (with it), the world seemed prosperous and safe, and the Backstreet Boys wanted it that way.

151

What way? Whatever way looked good with matching hats and synchronized twirls. By the end of the 1990s the growing college music scene had pushed through to a *bona fide* "alternative movement" with a whole range of anti-mainstream forces at work, from jangly pop/punk-lite to true independent rock. Sometimes we smashed pumpkins, sometimes we raged against the machine, but overall we led a semi-charmed kind of life. Did we party like it was 1999 in 1999? Not really. But we still stayed up all night because we didn't want to miss a thing.

1. In the 1992 movie *Singles*, Matt Dillon plays the lead singer of a fictional Seattle-based grunge band called Citizen Dick. The other members of his band in the movie are played by what real-life Seattle-based grunge band that notoriously boycotted Ticketmaster in the 1990s?

_____

Points: 1

2. He was born in South Africa, named his band after himself, and has "so much to say." Who is he?

a) Santana
b) Dave Matthews
c) Spencer Davis
d) Ben Folds
e) Jeff Beck

Points: 1

3. Weezer's lead singer and songwriter Rivers Cuomo studied at what prestigious New England University after his band's debut known as *The Blue Album*?

a) Yale
b) Harvard
c) Princeton
d) Smith
e) Brown

Points: 1

4. Which R.E.M. song from the early 1990s was the first number one song to use a mandolin since Rod Stewart's 1971 hit "Maggie May"?

a) "Losing My Religion"
b) "Shiny Happy People"
c) "Nightswimming"
d) "Country Feedback"
e) "It's the End of the World as We Know It"

Points: 1

5. The title of this Smashing Pumpkins song from *Mellon Collie and the Infinite Sadness* refers back to a year when Rod Stewart asked "Do Ya Think I'm Sexy?", Blondie hit number one in the U.S. for the first time with "Heart of Glass," and Kermit the Frog made a rainbow connection. What is Billy Corgan's song called?

Points: 1

6. What is the best-selling punk album of all time (if you consider these latecomers to the scene, from California's East Bay, to be punk and not punk-lite)?

a) *Smash* (The Offspring)
b) *Dookie* (Green Day)
c) *London Calling* (The Clash)
d) *Walk Among Us* (The Misfits)
e) *Leave Home* (The Ramones)

Points: 1

7. Her 1992 "Ain't It Heavy" and 1994 "Come To My Window" both earned her Grammys for Best Female Rock Vocal Performance. Who is she?

a) **Melissa Etheridge**
b) **Joss Stone**
c) **k.d. lang**
d) **Bonnie Raitt**
e) **Toni Braxton**

Points: 1

8. The 11th track on The Cranberries' second album *No Need to Argue* is a tribute to which Irish poet?

a) **William Butler Yeats**
b) **Oscar Wilde**
c) **Patrick Kavanagh**
d) **Trevor Joyce**
e) **Jonathan Swift**

Points: 1

9. What was the highest Billboard chart position in the U.S. for Oasis's number one (in the U.K.) album *Definitely Maybe*?

a) 1
b) 9
c) 58
d) 103
e) It didn't chart in the U.S.

Points: 1

10. Though millions of fans worldwide could die happy if he did, Morrissey has made it clear he would never want to join a reunion of The Smiths, and continues to blame the demise of the band on:

a) Johnny Marr
b) Mike Joyce
c) Andy Rourke
d) himself
e) "People who I'd much rather kick in the eye"

Bonus: When drummer Mike Joyce sued Morrissey and Johnny Marr citing unfair distribution of royalties (a case which he won), what was the breakdown among band members?

_____ **Morrissey**
_____ **Johnny Marr**
_____ **Mike Joyce**
_____ **Andy Rourke**

Points: 1 + Bonus: 2

11. Moments before he drowned in Wolf River Harbor, Jeff Buckley is said to have been singing the chorus of what Led Zeppelin song from their second album on which Jimmy Page used a backwards echo?

a) **"Black Dog"**
b) **"Houses of the Holy"**
c) **"Stairway to Heaven"**
d) **"Whole Lotta Love"**
e) **"Nobody's Fault But Mine"**

Points: 2

12. Quentin Tarantino cited this 1968 Dusty Springfield song as absolutely essential to the scene in *Pulp Fiction* (1994) where Vincent (John Travolta) is greeted by Mia (Uma Thurman) over the intercom in her building.

a) **"What Have I Done to Deserve This?"**
b) **"Son of a Preacher Man"**
c) **"I Only Want to Be With You"**
d) **"Surf Rider"**
e) **"Flowers on the Wall"**

Points: 1

13. Growing up in Alaska and singing with her dad, Jewel learned this unusual vocal technique said to have originated in the Swiss Alps. The same technique is celebrated in the song from *The Sound of Music* about a lonely goatherd. What is it?

Points: 1

14. On the famous September 1993 *Rolling Stone* magazine cover featuring a topless Janet Jackson, name one of the seven bands that are also listed on the cover.

Points: 1

15. This Canadian band had an early 1990s hit with "Brian Wilson," a reference to one of the Beach Boys. Their name alone might get them invited for free drinks at a happy hour, but once the bartender saw them they'd be bounced out like a rubber ball. What are they called?

Points: 1

16. This flower is native to North America and is also the name of Natalie Merchant's first solo album:

a) **Tigerlily**
b) **Ophelia**
c) **Desert Marigold**
d) **Moss Verbena**
e) **Jubilee**

Points: 1

17. What 80s band inspired the name Radiohead? (Hint: They're not pundits, but from the name they sound like they might be.)

_____

Points: 1

18. What band had a 1993 smash hit with the song "What's Up?" (Hint: In both style and name, the band was accused of ripping off Concrete Blond.)

_____

Points: 1

19. One new song was written for the film version of Andrew Lloyd Webber's musical *Evita*. What was it?

a) "You Must Love Me"
b) "My Heart Will Go On"
c) "Another Suitcase in Another Hall"
d) "Don't Cry for Me, Argentina"
e) "Nothing Fails"

Points: 1

20. According to the 1993 hit by the Swedish pop band Ace of Base, what was the only thing "she" wanted?

a) a trip across the world
b) another baby
c) another chance with her lover
d) a house with a picket fence
e) one last night together

Points: 1

21. Which folk-blues musician from Louisiana did Kurt Cobain refer to as his favorite performer on Nirvana's MTV Unplugged recording?

_____ **Belly**

Points: 1

22. Which of the following is *not* one of Boston hard-rockers Aerosmith's songs?

a) "Cryin'"
b) "Angel"
c) "Janie's Got a Gun"
d) "I Don't Want To Miss a Thing"
e) "Angie"

Points: 1

23. The Indigo Girls had a hit single in 1992 with "Galileo," which explored the concept of reincarnation. In the song, which fear does singer Emily Saliers blame on someone in a past life?

a) fear of flying
b) fear of motion
c) fear of heights
d) fear of being alone
e) fear of spiders

Points: 1

24. This celebrated Chinese-American architect designed The Rock and Roll Hall of Fame (as well as The Louvre Pyramid, Boston's J.F.K. Library and dozens of other landmark buildings). Who is he?

Points: 1

25. Name the film this line comes from and the character who said it.

"Did I listen to pop music because I was miserable? Or was I miserable because I listened to pop music?"

Movie: _____

Character: _____

Points: 1 for each correct answer

26. 'Round what month was the Counting Crows' album that contained the song "Round Here" along with the Billboard hit "Mr. Jones," named for?

_____

Points: 1

27. Dave Navarro, guitarist for Jane's Addiction, recorded one album (1995's *One Hot Minute*) with this experimental funk-rock band from L.A. What are they called?

_____

Points: 1

28. The video for which Grammy-award winning 1993 song opens with the caption: "I have travelled across the universe through the years to find her. Sometimes going all the way is just a start ..."

a) "Creep" (Radiohead)
b) "Runaway Train" (Soul Asylum)
c) "No Rain" (Blind Melon)
d) "I Would Do Anything for Love (But I Won't Do That)" (Meatloaf)
e) "Dream Lover" Mariah Carey

Points: 1

29. Name the film this line comes from and the character who said it:

"Are you doing what I told you? Are you thinking of that reed as a woman's nipple?"

Movie: _____

Character: _____

Points: 1 for each correct answer

30. The first version of Blink-182's *Enema of the State* album art used a symbol from a humanitarian organization that asked that it be removed. Which one was it?

a) Unicef
b) Project HOPE
c) Red Cross
d) Christian Mission Service
e) Food Not Bombs

Points: 2

31. Match the stars to their pre-celebrity gigs.

Madonna	Gas station attendant
Rod Stewart	Tax officer
Kelly Clarkson	Grave digger
Sting	Clerk at Dunkin' Donuts
Kurt Cobain	Hairdresser
Mary J. Blige	Promoted energy drinks
Eddie Vedder	Clerk at McDonald's
Shania Twain	Janitor

Points: 1 for each correct match

32. Which of the following songs is not on the *Reality Bites* soundtrack?

a) "My Sharona" (The Knack)
b) "Fools Like Me" (Lisa Loeb & Nine Stories)
c) "Locked Out" (Crowded House)
d) "I'm Nuthin'" (Ethan Hawke)
e) "Don't Turn Around" (Ace of Base)

Points: 1

33. The New Mexico church featured in the 1985 western *Silverado* is also used in what epic early 90s video starring model Stephanie Seymour?

Points: 1

34. Many people think this band, originally called Hybrid Theory, got their name from a park in Chicago, but it was actually inspired by one in Santa Monica, California. What are they called?

Points: 1

35. In which video from 1998's *Supposed Former Infatuation Junkie* did Canadian singer-songwriter Alanis Morissette appear to be naked surrounded by daily life on the streets, in the subway, and in the grocery store?

a) "Ironic"
b) "Uninvited"
c) "Thank U"
d) "Head Over Feet"
e) "You Oughta Know"

Points: 1

36. What hip hop/rap trio from New York is named after two everyday condiments?

_____

Bonus: The third member of the trio almost shares a name with which Disney heroine?

_____

Points: 1 + Bonus: 1

37. What was the name of the Nine Inch Nails tour that included Woodstock '94?

a) **Pretty Hate Machine**
b) **Fragility**
c) **With Teeth**
d) **Lights in the Sky**
e) **Self-Destruct**

Bonus: NIN lead singer Trent Reznor sang the back-up vocals on "Past the Mission," a song on which female artist's 1994 *Under the Pink* album?

Points: 2 + Bonus: 1

38. Stevie Van Zandt plays guitar with the E Street Band and also played Silvio Dante on which HBO Drama?

a) *Six Feet Under*
b) *Entourage*
c) *The Wire*
d) *Rome*
e) *The Sopranos*

Points: 1

39. Ten years after the power, pleasure, and pain of Seal's "Kiss from a Rose" stole the hearts of millions, the English R&B singer married this German supermodel.

a) **Gisele Bündchen**
b) **Janice Dickinson**
c) **Christie Brinkley**
d) **Heidi Klum**
e) **Linda Evangelista**

Points: 1

Score ___/51
Bonus ___/4
1990s Total ___/55

▶ 21st Century

(37 questions)

How will the first decade of the twenty-first century be remembered? It's hard to say. The millennium bug turned out to be about as harmful as a caterpillar, the digital revolution took over nearly every aspect of our lives, and reality shows became bigger than reality. We got to choose our own idols, bands worried more about ringtones than records, and despite repeated challenges from an English band that sounds quite a bit like Them, U2 made sure one thing it didn't leave behind in the new millennium was the title of world's biggest band.

Two of the most earth-shattering events happened at opposite ends of the decade. The country that for so long had been "undimmed by human tears" was attacked on September 11, 2001 in a catastrophic quadruple hijacking of commercial airliners, two of which destroyed New York City's Twin Towers. Worldwide sympathy was systematically overturned by the war in the Middle East, which began in 2003. In November 2008, the American people stopped waiting for the world to change and elected the first African-American President to office.

Now consigned to the "quaint nostalgia" bin: film cameras, walkmans, landlines, mix tapes, wondering if there's any way you can get in touch with a long-lost friend, concept albums, album art, and dial-up modems. More than ever we participate in cultural activities (like listening to music and watching movies) alone, yet at the same time advances in technology have paved the way for a democratic musical arena, where fans can easily share music, record their own, and watch their favorite vintage videos at will.

With the sudden death of Michael Jackson in 2009, the world lost one of its brightest (if most bizarre) stars. The disappearing act of the fifty-year-old man, who as a young boy had promised he'd be there whenever we needed him, marked the final and incontestable end to the childhood of the generation that had for so long refused to grow up.

1. What song, written in the 1940s and performed at President Obama's Inaugural Ball, is also the most popular song requested for a first dance at a wedding?

Points: 1

2. What *Cruel Intentions* actor appears in the beginning of Outkast's "Hey Ya" video?

a) **Ryan Phillipe**
b) **Justin Timberlake**
c) **Jamie Foxx**
d) **Will Smith**
e) **Harrison Ford**

Points: 2

3. At the 2001 Grammy Awards, Faith Hill, winner of three awards, thanked her parents for letting her see which legendary singer when she was eight years old? (Hint: She may have felt like she saw royalty.)

a) **David Bowie**
b) **Roy Orbison**
c) **Diana Ross**
d) **Joni Mitchell**
e) **Elvis Presley**

Points: 1

4. A favorite at sporting events, this calypso-inspired song with the catchy canine refrain won the 2000 Grammy for Best Dance Recording. What is it called?

_____

Points: 1

5. Match the album to the artist.

Gwen Stefani   *Love. Angel. Music. Baby.*

Justin Timberlake   *Blood Sugar Sex Magik*

Red Hot Chili   *FutureSex/LoveSounds*
   Peppers

Points: 2

6. In the video for "I'm Glad" from her 2002 album *This is Me ... Then*, Jennifer Lopez reenacted dance scenes from what iconic 1980s movie set in Pittsburgh, Pennsylvania?

a) *Footloose*
b) *Dirty Dancing*
c) *Flashdance*
d) *My Left Foot*
e) *She's Gotta Have It*

Points: 1

7. Number 49 on VH1's *Most Awesomely Bad Songs ... Ever* and number 84 on Billboard's Greatest Songs of All Time, Puff Daddy and Faith Evans' 1997 hit, "I'll Be Missing You," samples which 1983 song by The Police?

_____

Bonus: There's another sampled melody in there. What is it?

_____

Points: 1 + Bonus: 3

8. What was the controversial act featured on the cover of the Arctic Monkey's 2006 *Whatever People Say I Am, That's What I'm Not?*

a) fornication
b) flag burning
c) smoking
d) assassination
e) snorting coke

Points: 1

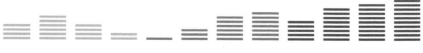

9. Rihanna's 2007 single "Umbrella" was the longest-running number one song in a decade. The 1994 hit that ran even longer, "Love Is All Around," was performed by a group that, judging by its name, may have been in serious need of an umbrella. What were they called?

_____

Bonus: What word does Rihanna have tattooed on her middle finger?

_____

Points: 1 + Bonus: 1

10. At various concerts Robbie Williams, Coldplay, and U2 all adopted a line from this alternative Las Vegas band's song "All These Things That I've Done." What is the name of the band that created the anthemic refrain? (Hint: Don't kill yourself trying to come up with the answer.)

Points: 1

11. The singer/actress who plays Hannah Montana is the real-life daughter of which country singer?

a) Billy Ray Cyrus
b) Garth Brooks
c) Keith Urban
d) Kenny Chesney
e) Toby Keith

Points: 1

12. Who holds The Guinness Book of World Record's title for "Highest-Grossing Music Tour By a Female Artist"? (Hint: The tour made over $250 million and said "farewell" in 2005.)

_____

Points: 1

13. In 2004, *Rolling Stone* magazine published what they considered "The 500 Greatest Songs of All Time." Only one of those songs is in a language other than English. The language is Spanish—what is the song?

_____

Points: 1

14. At the end of the infamous October 2004 *Saturday Night Live* episode when she first appeared as a musical guest, what did Ashlee Simpson say was the reason she did a jig during her rendition of "Pieces of Me"?

a) **She was sick and couldn't sing**
b) **Her band played the wrong song**
c) **Her microphone wasn't on**
d) **She lost her earpiece**
e) **The producers had asked her to lip sync**

Points: 1

15. In the 2002 film *8 Mile*, Jimmy is seen writing a song on a bus. The paper is the actual draft of which Eminem song?

a) "Lose Yourself"
b) "8 Mile"
c) "Stan"
d) "The Real Slim Shady"
e) "Like Toy Soldiers"

Points: 1

16. Record producer Phil Spector, convicted of second-degree murder in 2009, is best-known professionally for creating what sound technique?

Points: 1

17. Her name means "thankful" in Arabic, something this half-Colombian, half-Lebanese singer and dancer surely must have been when fans worldwide agreed that her hips didn't lie. What is her name?

Points: 1

18. Corey Hart of "I Wear My Sunglasses at Night" fame currently writes for this popular female artist:

a) **Celine Dion**
b) **Britney Spears**
c) **Lady GaGa**
d) **Jennifer Hudson**
e) **Gwen Stefani**

Points: 1

19. Two Rolling Stones' songs from 1967's *Between the Buttons* play during the film *The Royal Tenenbaums* (2001), but they do not appear on either release of the soundtrack. What are they? (Pick two.)

a) "Needle in the Hay"
b) "Look at Me"
c) "Ruby Tuesday"
d) "She Smiled Sweetly"
e) "Rock the Casbah"

Points: 2

20. In 2002, the daughter of celebrated Indian sitar player Ravi Shankar asked audiences to come away with her. Who is she?

a) **Shania Twain**
b) **Norah Jones**
c) **Faith Hill**
d) **Alicia Keys**
e) **Ani DiFranco**

Points: 1

21. Which short-lived but hugely popular file-sharing service was shut down as a result of legal issues kicked off by a challenge from Metallica, whose song "I Disappear" made its way across the peer-to-peer network before it was released?

a) Napster
b) Kazaa
c) Pandora
d) eDonkey2000
e) LiveWire

Points: 1

22. In the 2000 movie *Duets*, Gwyneth Paltrow sings which song made famous by Kim Carnes, referencing a movie star from Hollywood's Golden Era?

Points: 1

23. She played a friend of Rudy Huxtable's on an episode of *The Cosby Show*, as a teenager she left Columbia University to pursue music, and in 2008 she had the most popular song on the radio, when surely no one could get in the way of what she was feeling. Who is she?

a) Beyoncé
b) Gwen Stefani
c) Fergie
d) Alicia Keys
e) Mary J. Blige

Points: 1

24. In 2000, the Hard Rock Café in London auctioned which item previously owned by John Lennon for $2.1 million?

_____

Points: 1

25. Amy Winehouse's second studio album, which earned the singer four Grammys and the title "Best New Artist," has just one word different from the first album Australian hard rockers AC/DC recorded after the death of their lead singer, Bon Scott. What is the name of Amy Winehouse's album?

a) *Back to Black*
b) *Back in Black*
c) *Highway to Hell*
d) *Highway from Hell*
e) *The Razors Edge*

Points: 1

26. What song did Beyoncé perform in her first talent show? (Hint: Try to imagine her at seven years old.)

_____

Points: 1

27. Who wrote the words and music to the hit dance song "Get the Party Started" from Pink's 2001 album *Missundaztood?*

a) **Pink**
b) **Pat Benatar**
c) **Linda Perry**
d) **Janet Jackson**
e) **Berry Gordy**

Points: 1

28. Name the film this quote comes from and the character who said it.

"If you think Mick Jagger will still be out there trying to be a rock star at age fifty, then you are sadly, sadly mistaken."

Movie: _____

Character: _____

Points: 1 for each correct answer

29. The second track on U2's *All That You Can't Leave Behind* (2000) was written for Michael Hutchence, the Australian lead singer of INXS. What is the name of the song?

Points: 1

30. True or false?
For their 2007 album *In Rainbows*, Radiohead allowed fans to pay whatever they wished for a digital download, from zero on up.

Points: 1

31. Before she married dancer Kevin Federline, Britney Spears had a whirlwind first marriage to a friend from childhood that was annulled 55 hours after the couple married in which U.S. city?

_____

Bonus: Name a different star for whom Kevin Federline was a backup dancer.

_____

Points: 1 + Bonus: 1

32. Jay-Z makes a cameo appearance on "Lost!" the third single released from Coldplay's 2008 *Viva La Vida or Death and All His Friends*. In it, he references once towering but now fallen celebrities and historical figures. Who among the following list does he *not* reference?

a) Martin Luther King
b) Bobby Brown
c) Tupac Shakur
d) Caesar
e) Jam Master Jay

Points: 3

33. On Sigur Rós' 2002 album ( ), the songs are sung in which made-up language (often mistaken for, and with great similarities to, Icelandic)?

Points: 2

34. In January 2006, Kanye West drew criticism for dressing up like this religious figure on the cover of *Rolling Stone* magazine. The same figure is referenced in the title to the third single West released from his first album, *The College Dropout*.

Points: 1

35. Proving there was life after Zeppelin, Robert Plant teamed up with this country singer from Illinois for 2007's collaborative *Raising Sand*, which went on to win Grammys for Album and Record of the Year.

Points: 1

36. True or false?

The White Stripes Jack White and Meg White are brother and sister.

Bonus: The White Stripes' "Black Math" requires a fret which most guitars don't have. Which is it?

a) 22nd
b) 25th
c) 26th
d) 27th
e) 29th

Points: 1 + Bonus: 1

37. "Independent Women," "Survivor," and "Bootylicious" were all singles from a 2001 Destiny's Child album which shares the name with one of these three songs. Which one?

_____

Points: 1

Score ___/44
Bonus ___/6
21st Century Total ___/50

▶ Rock & Pop Challenge

(29 questions)

1. According to the Billboard Charts, which artist has the greatest number of Top 40 hits of all time?

a) The Beatles
b) Britney Spears
c) Madonna
d) Elvis Presley
e) Michael Jackson

Points: 1

2. Which artist won the greatest number of Grammys?

a) **Stevie Wonder**
b) **Bonnie Raitt**
c) **Diana Ross**
d) **Sting**
e) **Paul McCartney**

Points: 1

3. Fill in the blanks for the names of the following records.

a) **Guns N' Roses**   *Appetite for* _____
b) **Jimi Hendrix**   *Are You* _____
c) **The Band**   *Music from Big* _____
d) **Blondie**   _____ *Lines*
e) **Low**   *Things We* _____ *Fire*
f) **Beastie Boys**   *Licensed to* _____

Points: 1 for each correct answer

4. Who's that girl (or boy)?

a) **Bob Dylan**   **"Visions of _____"**
b) **Paul Simon**   **"You Can Call Me _____"**
c) **The Beatles**   **"_____ In the Sky with Diamonds"**
d) **Steely Dan**   **"_____ Don't Lose That Number"**
e) **Dexy's Midnight Runners** **"Come on _____"**
f) **The Velvet Underground**   **"Sweet _____"**

Points: 1 for each correct answer

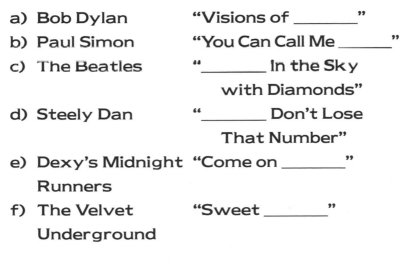

5. Match the band to their original name.

Chicago
Faith No More
U2
Creedence Clearwater Revival
a-ha
The Beatles
The Cranberries
Black Sabbath
The Eagles
Beastie Boys

Sharp Young Men

The Golliwogs

Cranberries Saw Us

The Quarrymen

Feedback

The Young Aborigines

Teen King and the Emergencies

Chicago Transit Authority

Spider Empire

Earth

Points: 1 for each correct match

6. Which day does Robert Smith not care about in "Friday I'm in Love"?

_____

Points: 1

7. For the Bangles, it's just another manic which day of the week?

_____

Points: 1

8. And Mick Jagger has to say goodbye to Ruby _____?

_____

Points: 1

9. In Billy Joel's "Piano Man," what time on Saturday does "the regular crowd shuffle in"?

_____

Points: 1

10. The same word is missing from these five song titles. What is it?

a) "November _____" (Guns N' Roses)
b) "Purple _____" (Prince)
c) "I Can't Stand the _____" (Tina Turner)
d) "Here Comes the _____ Again" (Eurythmics)

Points: 1

11. Check off the songs below which feature the same chord progression 1-5-6-4.

a) "With or Without You" (U2)
b) "Glycerine" (Bush)
c) "No Woman, No Cry" (Bob Marley)
d) "When I Come Around" (Green Day)
e) "Spiderwebs" (No Doubt)
f) "Superman" (Five for Fighting)
g) "She Will be Loved" (Maroon 5)
h) "Torn" (Natalie Imbruglia)
i) "So Lonely" (The Police)

Points: 4

12. Which of the following musicians is *not* left-handed?

a) Jimi Hendrix
b) Paul McCartney
c) Eddie Van Halen
d) Jimmy Cliff
e) Glenn Frey

Points: 1

13. Which of the following musicians *is* left-handed but only plays a standard guitar/bass?

a) **Jimi Hendrix**
b) **Paul McCartney**
c) **Eddie Van Halen**
d) **Jimmy Cliff**
e) **Glenn Frey**

Points: 1

14. Which of the following songs does *not* have its title as part of the first line?

a) **"Two Princes" (Spin Doctors)**
b) **"Black Magic Woman" (Santana)**
c) **"Scar Tissue" (Red Hot Chili Peppers)**
d) **"Everybody Hurts" (R.E.M.)**
e) **"Yesterday" (The Beatles)**

Points: 1

15. Famous Misheard Lyrics—what are they really saying?

a) Sounds like: "Wrapped up like a douche ..."
From "Blinded by the Light" (Bruce Springsteen)
Actual line: _____

b) Sounds like: "There's a bathroom on the right"
From "Bad Moon Rising" (Creedence Clearwater Revival)
Actual line: _____

c) Sounds like: "Hold me close, young Tony Danza"
From "Tiny Dancer" (Elton John)
Actual line: _____

d) Sounds like: "Might as well face it you're a d*ck with a glove"
From "Addicted to Love" (Robert Palmer)
Actual line: _____

e) Sounds like: "It doesn't make a difference if we're naked or not"
From "Livin' on a Prayer" (Bon Jovi)
Actual line: _____

Points: 1 for each correct answer

16. Which of the following songs does *not* feature a flute?

a) "Enlightenment" (Van Morrison)
b) "Dear Diary" (Moody Blues)
c) "In the Court of the Crimson King" (King Crimson)
d) "California Dreamin'" (The Mamas & The Papas)
e) "Living in the Past" (Jethro Tull)

Points: 1

17. When it comes to the Grammy Awards, the "Song of the Year" is awarded to

a) The song's performer
b) The song's performer and composer
c) The song's performer, composer, and production team
e) The song's composer
f) The record label

Points: 1

18. What do these musicians have in common?

David Bowie, Gene Simmons, Lou Reed, Billy Joel, Leonard Cohen, Bob Dylan, The Beastie Boys, Perry Farrell, The Ramones

Points: 1

19. At what age did these musicians die?

a) Sam Cooke _____
b) Ian Curtis (Joy Division) _____
c) Brian Jones (The Rolling Stones) _____
d) Janis Joplin _____
e) John Lennon _____
f) Notorious BIG _____
g) Selena _____
h) Ritchie Valens _____
i) Mozart _____

Points: 1 for each correct answer

20. Which two of the following song titles do not officially use a question mark?

a) "Why Do Fools Fall in Love" (Frankie Lymon & the Teenagers)
b) "Have You Ever Really Loved a Woman" (Bryan Adams)
c) "What's Going On" (Marvin Gaye)
d) "Are You Lonesome Tonight" (Elvis Presley)
e) "What's My Age Again" (Blink-182)

Points: 2

21. Fill in the state names in the following song titles.

a) _____ Dreamin' (The Mamas & The Papas)
b) _____ State of Mind (Billy Joel)
c) Yellow Rose of _____ (Mitch Miller)
d) Midnight Train to _____ (Gladys Knight and the Pips)
e) Sweet Home _____ (Lynyrd Skynyrd)

This one is a city:

f) _____ Calling (The Clash)

Points: 1 for each correct answer

22. Match the guitar hero with their "axe" of choice.

Peter Buck
Tomi Iommi
Eddie Van Halen
The Edge
Stevie Ray Vaughn
Slash
B.B. King
John Frusciante
Jimmy Page
Kurt Cobain
Keith Richards
Chuck Berry

Rickenbacker

Gibson SG with Laney amp

Fender Telecaster

Gibson ES-335

Stratocaster

Stratocaster or Vox

Gibson ES-335 with stereo outputs (Lucille)

Gibson Les Paul

Charvel

Fender Jag-stang

Gibson Les Paul or SG Double Neck

Stratocaster

Points: 1 for each correct match

23. The bands in the left-hand column took their names from songs by the artists in the right-hand column. Can you match the band name to the musician whose song inspired it?

Sisters of Mercy	**Bob Dylan**
Moody Blues	**Bing Crosby**
Simple Minds	**Leonard Cohen**
Deep Purple	**Duke Ellington**
Judas Priest	**David Bowie**

Points: 1 for each correct match

24. Match the artist with the song title.

Bo Bice	"Try A Little Tenderness"
Macy Gray	"Willing to Try"
Paul McCartney	"One More Try"
A1	"Try Not To Cry"
Glen Campbell	"I Try"

Points: 1 for each correct match

25. What do the following songs have in common?

a) "Thunder Road" (Bruce Springsteen)
b) "Hey" (Pixies)
c) "Let It Be" (The Beatles)
d) "Proud Mary" (Creedence Clearwater Revival)
e) "Just Like a Woman" (Bob Dylan)

Points: 1

26. What animals are pictured on the front covers of the following albums?

a) *Odeley* (Beck) _____
b) *Get a Grip* (Aerosmith) _____
c) *Pet Sounds* (The Beach Boys) _____
d) *Crazy Horse* (Neil Young) _____

Points: 1 for each correct answer

27. Which one of the following bands did *not* have actual brothers as band members?

a) Oasis
b) The Allman Brothers Band
c) The Bee Gees
d) AC/DC
e) The Righteous Brothers
f) The Jackson 5
g) Jonas Brothers

Points: 2

28. Match the solo artists with the band they came from.

Peter Gabriel	Them
Robert Plant	The Faces
Van Morrison	Genesis
Peter Frampton	Led Zeppelin
Ted Nugent	Amboy Dukes
Rod Stewart	The Herd and Humble Pie

Points: 1 for each correct match

29. Timed Test. Set your stop watch for 60 seconds. Can you supply the real (commonly used, if not birth) names of the rock and pop stars below?

King of Pop _____

The King _____

King of the 12-string guitar _____

The Edge _____

Slash _____

The Boss _____

Bono _____

The Fab Four _____

Man in Black _____

The Lizard King _____

Lady Soul _____

Godmother of Punk _____

The Fab Five _____

O(+> _____

Points: 1 for each correct answer

Rock & Pop Challenge Score ___/110

▶ For Music Geeks

(20 questions)

There are the music geeks who collect one-time vinyl release imports from unsigned bands and toss around names of riot grrrl bands, and then there are the seriously geeky music aficionados—the ones who played in the orchestra, understand harmony and pitch, and know the difference between the Dorian and Lydian modes. This section is for the latter, those who prefer Beethoven to Malkmus and never got much indie cred for being true devotees of rhythm and melody.

1. Which musical instrument is the best-selling worldwide?

a) keyboard
b) acoustic guitar
c) recorder
d) electric guitar
e) harmonica

Points: 1

2. It's the birthplace of the compact disc, but Japan's national instrument hasn't caught on in quite the same way. What is it?

a) **tsuzumi**
b) **shamisen**
c) **shakuhachi**
d) **koto**
e) **horagai**

Points: 3

3. What U.S. East Coast city is home to the biggest and loudest instrument ever made, the Auditorium Organ, completed in 1932 and taking up more than 15 million cubic feet.

a) **Portland, Maine**
b) **Boston, Massachusetts**
c) **New York, New York**
d) **Atlantic City, New Jersey**
e) **Charleston, South Carolina**

Points: 2

4. Which is the fastest of the following tempos?

a) Adagio
b) Allegro
c) Largo
d) Lento
e) Moderato

Points: 1

5. Originally performed in the weeks leading up to Easter, this oratorio by George Frideric Handel is now most closely associated with Christmas when its "Hallelujah Chorus" is often played. What is the name of this eighteenth-century work?

a) *The Book of Revelation*
b) *Adeste Fideles*
c) *The Passion*
d) *The Messiah*
e) *Ode to Joy*

Points: 1

6. For his first solid-body guitar, what did Les Paul use for pickups?

a) **telephone parts**
b) **coke bottle caps**
c) **metal buttons**
d) **screws**
e) **metal scraps from a fender**

Points: 1

7. In 1977, The American Music Conference designated two instruments as the hardest to play. Which two of the following did they select?

a) bagpipe
b) 12-string guitar
c) oboe
d) drums
e) French horn

Points: 4

8. The conga, the samba, the tango, the rumba, and bossa nova are all music styles and what else?

a) instruments
b) islands in the West Indies
c) holidays in Brazil
d) dances
e) martial arts

Points: 1

9. Match the scales to the number of notes in each.

Diatonic	**12**
Pentatonic	**8**
Chromatic	**5**

Points: 3

10. How many keyboards does the organ at Westminster Abbey have?

_____

Points: 2

11. How old was Wolfgang Amadeus Mozart when he first published a Minuet and Trio in G?

_____

Points: 2

12. Requiem, the music for a memorial mass, is Latin for:

a) remember
b) resurrect
c) peace
d) rest
e) angel

Points: 1

13. In 1991, Plácido Domingo set a record for applause. The audience clapped for one hour and 20 minutes. What performance had the Spanish tenor taken part in?

a) *La Traviata* (Verdi)
b) *La Bohème* (Puccini)
c) *Otello* (Zeffirelli)
d) *Lohengrin* (Wagner)

Points: 2

14. Lincoln Center's Metropolitan Opera House has what basic shape, echoing early opera houses in Venice?

a) horseshoe
b) semi-circle
c) rectangle
d) triangle
e) octagon

Points: 1

15. Ludwig van Beethoven only wrote one opera. What is it called?

a) *Fidelio*
b) *The Marriage of Figaro*
c) *La Vestale*
d) *Madame Butterfly*
e) *Aida*

Points: 1

16. Name the movie which the following quote comes from and the character who said it.

"Sire, only opera can do this. In a play if more than one person speaks at the same time, it's just noise, no one can understand a word. But with opera, with music … with music you can have twenty individuals all talking at the same time, and it's not noise, it's a perfect harmony!"

Movie: _____

Character: _____

Points: 1 for each correct answer

17. Who was the most prolific composer of all time?

_____

Points: 2

18. Pyotr Ilyich Tchaikovsky wrote the music to which ballet (now a Christmas tradition) based on the story from E.T.A. Hoffman (adapted by Alexandre Dumas)?

a) *Swan Lake*
b) *Sleeping Beauty*
c) *Le Corsaire*
d) *Romeo and Juliet*
e) *The Nutcracker*

Points: 1

19. Put these instruments in order from high to low sounds:

a) Viola
b) Double Bass
c) Cello
d) Bass
e) Violin

Points: 3

20. The national anthem of which country begins with the following line (translated into English): "Let's go, children of the fatherland"?

a) Germany
b) France
c) Poland
d) Russia
e) Morocco

Points: 1

For Music Geeks Score ___/35

▶ Answers

Pre-rock 'n' roll

1. "Pomp and Circumstance, March No. 1"
2. Jazz
3. *Swing:* Glenn Miller, *Baroque:* Johann Sebastian Bach, *Bebop:* Charlie Parker *Classical:* Joseph Haydn, *Folk:* Joan Baez, *Blues:* Bessie Smith
4. Duck
5. a) LP
6. c) Blue
7. Glenn Miller
8. a) Nashville
9. "This Land Is Your Land"
10. d) *Holiday Inn*
11. c) tin foil
12. *Oklahoma!*
13. *The Phantom of the Opera* (Andrew Lloyd Webber)
14. *Les Misérables* (Claude-Michel Schönbergand and Alain Boubil)

15. Dorothy (Frances Ethel Gumm's stage name was Judy Garland)

1950s

1. Goodnight
2. d) *Love Me Tender*
3. Music Died
4. *Movie: Back to the Future, Character:* Marty McFly
5. The Kingston Trio
6. b) the Arkansas floods
7. Screamin' Jay Hawkins
8. False. Elvis had an *identical* twin named Jesse Garon who died before birth.
9. d) The Platters
10. a) "Walkin' After Midnight"

1960s

1. a) The Four Seasons
2. Taking Care of Business
3. e) The Supremes
4. Oh ("Oh, Pretty Woman")
5. b) 3
6. d) The Cure
7. The Monkees
8. b) 13
9. b) The Rolling Stones

10. b) Decca Records
11. b) James Brown
12. The Doors
    Bonus: c) bass
13. *Sgt. Pepper's Lonely Hearts Club Band* (The Beatles)
14. "(Sittin' On) The Dock of the Bay"
15. Simon and Garfunkel
16. c) Bob Dylan
17. Paul McCartney
18. d) 29 (Ringo Starr was born in July of 1940)
19. e) The Grateful Dead
20. a) True, b) True, c) False, it was from a Muddy Waters song, d) False, it was a cover of Chuck Berry's "Come On"
21. a) Jimi Hendrix
22. e) "Tambourine Man" (The Byrds)
23. b) The Yardbirds
24. d) Blood, Sweat & Tears
25. b) $18
26. Motown Records
27. d) Paris, France
28. c) the Army Airborne
29. Creedence Clearwater Revival
30. c) polio
31. d) horn

32. a) good
33. a) "America"
34. Charles Manson
35. December, 1963
36. Woodstock
37. d) Bob Dylan
38. Kennedy Airport, New York
39. d) Ray and Dave's sister
40. "Like a Rolling Stone"
41. Pearl

1970s

1. Asbury Park, South Jersey (Springsteen's *Greetings from Asbury Park* actually came out one year prior to the club's opening)
2. d) slide guitar
3. d) 21st
4. d) John Denver
5. Queen
6. David Bowie
7. The Hustle
8. "Bridge Over Troubled Water" (Simon and Garfunkel)
9. d) He overslept and missed an exam
10. Aretha Franklin (she's had 20 R&B/hip hop hits)
11. *The Who Sings My Generation*

12. d) Sid Vicious
    Bonus: 100
13. (a) Wild, (b) See, (c) Killing me, (d) Were, (e) Please
14. Keytar
15. *A Night at the Opera* and *A Day at the Races*
16. Bernie Taupin
17. Knotts Berry Farm amusement park in L.A.
18. Van Morrison
19. It was all men.
20. a) women's underwear
21. c) Eric Clapton
22. b) Coney Island High

23. d) Patti Smith
24. a) George Harrison
    Bonus: *Layla and Majnun*
25. e) *The Dark Side of the Moon* (Pink Floyd)
26. b) clavinet
27. Brenda and Eddie
28. The Bee Gees
29. c) "Auld Lang Syne"
30. True
31. b) 9:06 (the single was released at 4:41)
32. ABBA
    Bonus: Benny Andersson, Agnetha Fältskog, Anni-Frid Lyngstad and Björn Ulvaeus

33. d) airship (Led Zeppelin)
34. c) Martin Scorcese
35. Hawaii
36. e) *Hiding on the Backstreets*
37. False, it was written for the band's former lead singer, Syd Barrett, who died in 2006
38. c) Mick Fleetwood (drummer)
39. d) Andy Warhol
40. Crazy
41. a) Iggy Pop
42. *Oye Como Va*
43. A minor

Bonus: b) About halfway through
44. b) telling a woman not to cry

1980s

1. Michael Jackson's 1982 *Thriller* (over 47 million worldwide sales)
2. e) The Arrows
3. b) Bryan Adams
4. c) *Dreams*
5. c) "Plainsong"
6. a) *Dirty Dancing*
7. a) "Another One Bites the Dust" (Queen), b) "I Love Rock 'n' Roll (Joan Jett, originally,

The Arrows), c) "I Think We're Alone Now" (Tiffany, originally Tommy James & the Shondells), d) "Bad" (Michael Jackson), e) "Like a Virgin" (Madonna)

8. d) pink

9. red, gold, and green

10. d) San Pedro

11. George Michael

12. b) 1982

13. a) Duran Duran

14. c) "Africa"

15. b) 2nd word, d) 4th word

16. the drum machine

17. b) Sunday

18. a) Living Colour

19. *band:* Mötley Crüe, *drummer:* Tommy Lee Jones

20. e) the Italian horror film *I Tre Volti Della Paura*

21. d) Barry Manilow

22. Tina Turner

23. d) ribs

24. a) Rapid Eye Movement (R.E.M), b) Electric Light Orchestra (ELO), c) Orchestral Manoeuvres in the Dark (OMD), d) Unemployment

Benefit, Form 40 (UB40)

25. "All Night Long (All Night)"

26. d) Courtney Cox

27. a) Elvis Presley, b) Willie Nelson, e) David Hasselhoff

28. *1986 True Blue:* 21 million, *1984 Like a Virgin:* 19 million, *1998 Ray of Light:* 14 million, *1989 Like a Prayer:* 13 million, *1992 Erotica:* 5 million
Bonus: 1983 Madonna (her first album)

29. e) Rick Allen

30. d) wolf
Bonus: b) Sri Lanka

31. Casey Kasem

32. c) Kelley Deal (The Breeders)

33. b) "Where the Streets Have No Name"

34. a) One-quarter

35. Elvis Costello

36. d) The CIA

37. *Artist:* Cyndi Lauper, *Video:* "Girls Just Want to Have Fun"

38. b) "Foolish Beat"

39. The night
Bonus: d) the airport
Double Bonus: 30 mph

40. c) 1981

Bonus: August 1

41. d) "Take on Me" (a-ha)

42. "Dirty Laundry"

43. Ladies Love Cool James

Bonus: *Mama Said Knock You Out*

44. b) Sony

45. *For Those About To Rock (We Salute You)*

46. Strawberry Fields

47. c) 2

Bonus: "Don't Look Back in Anger"

48. e), the only video shot in all-color from *Slippery When Wet*

was "You Give Love a Bad Name"

49. Summer Olympics

1990s

1. Pearl Jam

2. b) Dave Matthews

3. b) Harvard

4. a) "Losing My Religion"

5. 1979

6. b) *Dookie* (Green Day)

7. a) Melissa Etheridge

8. a) William Butler Yeats (in the song "Yeat's Grave")

9. c) 58

10. a) Johnny Marr

Bonus: 40% each for Morrissey and Marr. 10% each for Joyce and bassist Andy Rourke

11. d) "Whole Lotta Love"
12. b) "Son of a Preacher Man"
13. yodeling
14. Stone Temple Pilots, Nirvana, Snow, Red Hot Chili Peppers, Radiohead, Bjork, or Buffalo Tom
15. Barenaked Ladies
16. a) Tigerlily
17. Talking Heads (with their song "Radio Head")
18. 4 Non Blondes
19. a) "You Must Love Me"
20. b) another baby
21. Lead
22. e) "Angie"
23. b) fear of motion
24. I.M. Pei
25. *Movie: High Fidelity, Character:* Rob Gordon
26. August
27. Red Hot Chili Peppers
28. d) "I Would Do Anything for Love (But I Won't Do That)" (Meatloaf)
29. *Movie: The Commitments,*

Character: Joey "the lips" Fagan

30. c) Red Cross

31. *Madonna:* Clerk at Dunkin' Donuts, *Rod Stewart:* Grave digger, *Kelly Clarkson:* Promoted energy drinks, *Sting:* Tax officer, *Kurt Cobain:* Janitor, *Mary J. Blige:* Hairdresser, *Eddie Vedder:* Gas station attendant, *Shania Twain:* Clerk at McDonald's

32. "Don't Turn Around" (Ace of Base)

33. "November Rain" Guns N' Roses

34. Linkin Park

35. c) "Thank U"

36. Salt-n-Pepa
Bonus: Cinderella

37. e) Self-Destruct Tour
Bonus: Tori Amos

38. e) *The Sopranos*

39. d) Heidi Klum

21st Century

1. "At Last," written by Mack Gordon and Harry Warren, popularized by Etta James

2. a) Ryan Phillipe

3. e) Elvis Presley

4. "Who Let The Dogs Out" (Baha Men)
5. *Gwen Stefani:* Love. Angel. Music. Baby, *Justin Timberlake:* FutureSex/Love-Sounds, *Red Hot Chili Peppers:* Blood Sugar Sex Magik
6. c) *Flashdance*
7. "Every Breath You Take"
   Bonus: The gospel hymn, "I'll Fly Away"
8. c) smoking
9. Wet Wet Wet
   Bonus: LOVE
10. The Killers

11. a) Billy Ray Cyrus
12. Cher, for The Farewell Tour, which finally said goodbye in 2005
13. "La Bamba" (Ritchie Valens)
14. b) Her band played the wrong song
15. a) "Lose Yourself"
16. the "wall of sound"
17. Shakira
18. a) Celine Dion
19. c) "Ruby Tuesday", d) "She Smiled Sweetly"
20. b) Norah Jones
21. a) Napster
22. "Bette Davis Eyes"
23. d) Alicia Keys

24. His Steinway piano
25. a) *Back to Black*
26. "Imagine" (John Lennon)
27. c) Linda Perry
28. *Movie: Almost Famous* (2000), *Character:* Dennis Hope
29. "Stuck in a Moment You Can't Get Out Of"
30. True
31. Las Vegas
    Bonus: Justin Timberlake/Gwen Stefani/Pink/Michael Jackson
32. e) Jam Master Jay

33. Vonlenska or Hopelandic
34. Jesus
35. Alison Krauss
36. False, they are a divorced couple.
    Bonus: e) 29th
37. Survivor

Rock & Pop Challenge

1. d) Elvis Presley
2. a) Stevie Wonder (20 Grammys)
3. a) Destruction, b) Experienced?, c) Pink, d) Parallel, e) Lost in the, f) III
4. a) Johanna, b) Al, c) Lucy,

d) Rikki, e) Eileen,
f) Jane

5. *Chicago:* Chicago
Transit Authority,
Faith No More: Sharp
Young Men, *U2:*
Feedback, *Creedence
Clearwater Revival:*
The Golliwogs, *a-ha:*
Spider Empire, *The
Beatles:* The
Quarrymen, *The
Cranberries:*
Cranberries Saw Us,
Black Sabbath: Earth,
The Eagles: Teen King
and the Emergencies,
Beastie Boys: The
Young Aborigines

6. Thursday
7. Monday
8. Tuesday
9. 9 o'clock
10. Rain
11. All of them
12. c) Eddie Van Halen
13. e) Glenn Frey
14. d) "Everybody Hurts"
(R.E.M.)
15. a) "Revved up like a
deuce", b) "There's a
bad moon on the
rise", c) "Hold me
closer, tiny dancer",
d) "Might as well
face it, you're
addicted to love", e)
"It doesn't make a

difference if we make it or not"

16. a) "Enlightenment" (Van Morrison)

17. e) The song's composer

18. They're all Jewish

19. a) Sam Cooke: 33, b) Ian Curtis (Joy Division): 23, c) Brian Jones (The Rolling Stones): 27, d) Janis Joplin: 27, e) John Lennon: 40, f) Notorious BIG: 24, g) Selena: 23, h) Ritchie Valens: 17, i) Mozart: 35

20. a) "Why Do Fools Fall in Love" (Frankie Lymon & the Teenagers), c) "What's Going On" (Marvin Gaye)

21. a) California, b) New York, c) Texas, d) Georgia, e) Alabama, f): London

22. *Peter Buck:* Rickenbacker, *Tomi Iommi:* Gibson SG with Laney Amp, *Eddie Van Halen:* Charvel, *The Edge:* Stratocaster or Vox, *Stevie Ray Vaughn:* Stratocaster, *Slash:*

Gibson Les Paul, *B.B. King:* Gibson ES-335 with stereo outputs (Lucille), *John Frusciante:* Stratocaster, *Jimmy Page:* Gibson Les Paul or SG Double Neck, *Kurt Cobain:* Fender Jag-stang, *Keith Richards:* Fender Telecaster, *Chuck Berry:* Gibson ES-335

23. *Sisters of Mercy:* Leonard Cohen, *Moody Blues:* Duke Ellington (song "Mood Indigo"), *Simple Minds:* David Bowie (song "Jean Genie"), *Deep Purple:* Bing Crosby, *Judas Priest:* Bob Dylan (song "The Battle of Frankie Lee and Judas Priest")

24. *Bo Bice:* "Willing to Try", *Macy Gray:* "I Try", *Paul McCartney:* "Try Not To Cry", *A1:* "One More Try", *Glen Campbell:* "Try A Little Tenderness"

25. They all contain the name Mary

26. a) dog, b) cow, c) goats, d) dog

27. e) The Righteous Brothers

28. *Peter Gabriel:* Genesis, *Robert Plant:* Led Zeppelin, *Van Morrison:* Them, *Peter Frampton:* The Herd and Humble Pie, *Ted Nugent:* Amboy Dukes, *Rod Stewart:* The Faces

29. *King of Pop:* Michael Jackson, *The King:* Elvis Presley, *King of the 12-string guitar:* Leadbelly, *The Edge:* David Evans, *Slash:* Saul Hudson, *The Boss:* Bruce Springsteen, *Bono:* Paul Hewson, *The Fab Four:* The Beatles, *Man in Black:* Johnny Cash, *The Lizard King:* Jim Morrison, *Lady Soul:* Aretha Franklin, *Godmother of Punk:* Patti Smith, *The Fab Five:* Duran Duran, *O(+>:* Prince (Prince Nelson)

For Music Geeks

1. e) harmonica
2. d) koto
3. d) Atlantic City, New Jersey
4. b) Allegro
5. d) *The Messiah*

6. a) telephone parts
7. c) oboe, e) French horn
8. d) dances
9. Pentatonic: 5, Diatonic: 8, Chromatic: 12
10. five
11. four
12. d) rest
13. c) *Otello* (Zeffirelli)
14. a) horseshoe
15. a) *Fidelio*

16. *Movie: Amadeus, Character:* Mozart
17. Georg Philipp Telemann (1681-1767) (over 3,000 compositions in total, although many were lost in World War II)
18. e) *The Nutcracker*
19. e) Violin, a) Viola, c) Cello, d) Bass, b) Double bass
20. b) France

▶ Scoring

It's up to you whether you want to compare your answers with the Answers section as you go, or wait until you've worked through an entire section or even the whole book. Once you've checked your answers, total up your points for each section then record your scores in the chart opposite to get your final tally.

Section	Total Possible	Your Score
Pre rock 'n' roll	25	___
1950s	20	___
1960s	70	___
1970s	60	___
1980s	75	___
1990s	55	___
21st Century	50	___
Rock & Pop Challenge	110	___
For Music Geeks	35	___
TOTAL SCORE	**500**	___

Now for the moment of reckoning. If you scored:

400 points or more
"We Are the Champions"

You loved turntables before they had any underground cachet and you kept making mix tapes long after they lost all of theirs. Chances are you play an instrument yourself, and you're as comfortable rattling off Grammy award-sweepers and chart-toppers as remembering limited release B-sides from unknown bands, reciting liner notes, and reading sheet music. Whether it's doo wap, hip hop, power pop, punk, metal, or folk, the only sound you like better than the clack of CDs in bins at the record store or the jangle of coins plummeting into the juke box, is the sound of music itself, the first thing you turn on when you wake up, and the last thing you hear as you're drifting off to sleep at night, if you can even bring yourself to turn it off. If nothing else, hopefully the quiz will let you sleep that much better, knowing you do in fact know *everything* and can now feel free to indulge in *High Fidelity*-like-disdain for those poor uncultured souls who don't own the essential albums of every generation,

300-399 points
"Rock and Roll All Night"

From your impressive score it's obvious you really know your Bohemian rhapsodies, summertime blues, and jailhouse rock. With all that you listen to and remember, you've probably spent hours doing the moonwalk, the twist, and la bamba, all while making confessions from the dance floor. Sure there may be the odd concert you forgot, album whose name slips your tongue, band you never could bring yourself to listen to, or even decade that is largely a fog (whether you lived through it or not), but you're a true music fan, conversant with everything from bluegrass to Garage Rock Revival, and of course you can always be counted on to stay for one more song.

200-299 points
"(Try) Just a Little Bit Harder"

You may not always have found what you were looking for, but you likely got a lot of satisfaction answering a multitude of questions without any help. If you put a little more (elbow) grease into it, you'd be the rock 'n' roll party queen (or king). You're familiar with a wide range of genres and eras, and your friends rely on you for upbeat cocktail party chatter full of clever pop cultural references and charged discussions of cool new bands. You may not remember every left-handed guitarist that played for only one tour with a post-punk second British Invasion power-ballad-happy-hair-band before OD'ing on heroin, but you can create the perfect soundtrack for any occasion and instantly recite brilliant lines from 80s love songs that capture the awkwardness or beauty or nostalgia of almost any situation.

100-199 points

"Darkness on the Edge of Town"

There are a few bands and years that really light your fire and once in a while there's a whole lot of shakin' going on. For the most part though, you're a little dazed and confused when it comes to remembering who sang what, who played what, and what a song was called, let alone what the real lyrics were or what the singer did after his fifteen minutes of fame were over. You've got your favorite albums and musical idols, and maybe you loved rock concerts and high school dances, but for now you're more likely to tell someone to "turn that down" than to put another dime in the juke box. Still, that doesn't mean you don't appreciate good vibrations as much as the magnificent sounds of silence after a hard day's night.

0-99 points
"Got to Give It Up"

Well, not really. Maybe you can just pay a little more attention next time you're conducting a search on iTunes or come across a copy of *Spin* magazine. No one could really have expected you to know who wrote *The Nutcracker* or what B.B. King called his Gibson ES-355. Sure, if Mark Antony really needed to know and LL Cool J was going to knock you out you might have pushed yourself to get jiggy with it, but when it comes to music, you're just as happy cruising along with one headlight and maybe once every twenty questions or so feeling that satisfying certainty that you know the answer. Plus you don't have to know who wrote it or what it meant to enjoy the music on in the background, whether it's a song generally agreed to be an all-time-great-the-sky-would-fall-in-if-this-record-didn't-exist piece of music history, or just your neighbor plunking out a few notes on an out-of-tune piano. And that doesn't mean you can't have

295

your idols, ones that defined a period in your life just as much as they did for anyone else, whether you asked them to hit it baby one more time, or had somewhere else you had to go.